THE
Winter
Garden

THE
Winter
Garden

Structure, planting and romance in the garden in winter

ELUNED PRICE

PHOTOGRAPHS BY CLIVE NICHOLS

SMITHMARK

In memory of my beloved parents
Corinne and Justin Price
who taught me how to look

*"Thou hast set all the borders of the earth;
thou hast made summer and winter"*

A SALAMANDER BOOK

© Salamander Books Ltd, 1996

9 8 7 6 5 4 3 2 1

This edition published in 1996 by
SMITHMARK Publishers,
a division of U. S. Media Holdings, Inc.,
16 East 32nd Street,
New York, NY 10016

ISBN 0-8317-6266-7

SMITHMARK Books are available for bulk purchase for sales promotion and premium use. For details write or call the manager of special sales, SMITHMARK Publishers,
16 East 32nd Street, New York,
NY 10016; (212) 532-6600.

Acknowledgements
To Clive who suggested it; Jo Smith and Richard Collins at Salamander who appreciated it; Benet who checked it; Philippa, Sylvia, Stephanie and Christopher who put up with my whingeing about it; Alan, my ex-husband, who supported it; and my darling daughters, Alex and Abi, who ignored it.

Credits
Editor: Joanna Smith
Designer: John Heritage
Colour Separation by P & W Graphics PTE Ltd, Singapore
Printed in Italy

Captions
Front endpaper: Winter aconites and snowdrops.
Back endpaper: Grass border at The Old Vicarage, Norfolk.
Page 1 *Hamamelis* x *intermedia* 'Diane'.
Page 3 Herbaceous border at The Old Rectory, Berkshire.
Page 5 *Malus toringo*.

All photographs © Clive Nichols, except:
p111 – Larix © Adrian Bloom
p113 – Magnolia © John Glover/Garden Picture Library
p118 – Populus © Andrew Lawson
Back jacket flap – Portrait of Eluned Price by Rob Brown

The photographer and publisher would like to thank the individuals concerned for allowing photography at the following locations:

p2/3, 45 (top), 71: The Old Rectory, Berkshire
p11, 74-77: The Dingle, Powys
p12/13: Parnham House, Dorset
p15: Cornwell Manor, Oxfordshire
p18: Barnsley House, Gloucestershire
p20-25: Wollerton Old Hall, Shropshire
p26-29: Gatacre Park, Shropshire
p30-33, 44: Hazelbury Manor, Wiltshire
p34-39, 72: Chenies Manor House, Buckinghamshire
p40/41: Painswick Rococo Garden, Gloucestershire
p42: Denmans, West Sussex
p43 (top): Chiffchaffs, Dorset
p43 (left), 68, 73: White Windows, Hampshire
p45 (bottom): East Lambrook Manor, Somerset
p46-48: Benington Lordship, Hertfordshire
p49-51, front endpaper: The Dower House, Gloucestershire
p58-60, back endpaper: Alan Gray and Graham Robeson,
  The Old Vicarage, Norfolk
p70, 82-85: Rousham House, Oxfordshire
p78-81: Heale Gardens, Wiltshire
p86-89: Mr and Mrs Coote, Osler Road, Oxford
p90: Brook Cottage, Oxfordshire

Photographic notes
The photographs in this book were taken over a period of seven years using three different camera systems.

The majority of the plant portraits were taken with an Olympus OM2 camera using a 90mm Macro lens. Because many winter flowers are very small, I was often forced to use extension tubes for increased magnification. The small apertures and long exposures required meant waiting around until days when there was no wind at all.

For scenic shots, I used two medium format cameras – a Bronica SQA and a Pentax 6x7. The Bronica produces square 6x6cm images, whereas the Pentax gives rectangular 6x7cm images. Both cameras create photographs which retain superb sharpness even when blown-up to a full page.

All the pictures in the book were taken on Fujichrome Velvia (50 ISO) film. This amazing film is especially suited to winter garden photography because of its biting sharpness, rich reds and blues and clear whites.

The films were processed by Colour Processing Laboratories, Reading, England.

CONTENTS

INTRODUCTION

6

STRUCTURE IN THE WINTER GARDEN

12

PLANTING IN THE WINTER GARDEN

40

ROMANCE IN THE WINTER GARDEN

68

THE PLANT DIRECTORY

90

INDEX

128

INTRODUCTION

Every season has its delights. The green sap of spring rises in young leaves hatched into life on an old tree, in plump buds bursting into flower, in the evanescent scent of bluebells lying in shards of a broken blue sky on the woodland floor, and in baby ducklings on their first outing with their mother.

Summer with the languor of heat, blowsy with ripe blooms, is short on water and long on hours of daylight. Only when I moved back to England from Scotland did I appreciate the rare joy of being able to garden until midnight, wrestling with the annual inexorable invasion of ground elder from the other side of the stone wall that separated our garden from the roe deer. Both were indefatigable: if the ground elder did not suffocate the roses, the roe deer would eat them. All the long evening dogs and children would run back and forth, trampling seedlings or damming the burn. They were oblivious of time, heedless of calls to bed, and who could blame them? I had raised them on Robert Louis Stevenson's *A Child's Garden of Verses*:

> 'And does it not seem hard to you
> When all the sky is clear and blue
> And I should like so much to play
> To have to go to bed by day?'

They used to quote it back at me. I hadn't a leg to stand on.

With autumn come trees heavy with fruit and the rosy blush of late blooms, then the crackle of fire leaves underfoot, the hissing of damp bon-

fires, an enfeebled sun obliterated by rising mists, and sinister hints of a hard time to come.

But winter is not such a bad thing. There is a magic in the tracery of spun silver cobwebs threaded from branch to branch, diamonds of ice suspended from its fragility; there is sorcery in the white whirl of wild clematis conjured along the hedgerows; mesmerism in the regular creak of snow compacting under your boots. There is a beauty even in its very bleakness, a sense of appropriateness to the season. Like the Japanese

Sapphire skies above copper bands in autumn's last fling in the beechwoods (right) and the winter gold of *Iris danfordiae* set in winter's crystal (below left).

concept of fusoki-shugi – the aesthetic of incompleteness, the perception of beauty in what has been left out rather than what has been included, the knowledge of what is to come or what is no more – it makes the appreciation of winter all the sharper.

An abundance of summer flowers, like a suntan to a person, makes any garden look good. But only in its winter pallor can you see the underlying bone structure: if that is handsome the rest will follow. And quite different rules apply when you assess a winter garden: it's no good looking for bouquets of borders and fecund foliage offset by a sharp emerald sward. Lacking the glorious Technicolor of autumn and the vibrancy of spring and summer, winter colour when it does appear

The serenity of an agricultural landscape in winter with rising mists and soft light is without par (right).

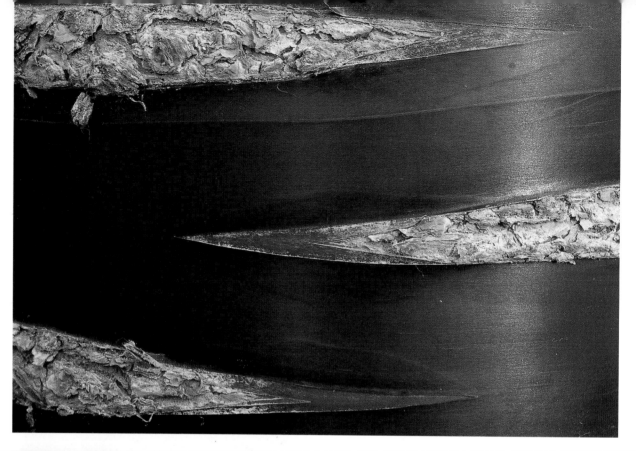

Some of winter's riches:
the bark of *Prunus serrula*
(above right) and *Camellia
sasanqua* (right).

draws all the more attention. It brings about a heightened perception, throwing into focus the simplicity of tiny yellow trumpets of jasmine on twiggy stems, magnifying the thin high scents of pale florets of viburnum in place of the designer perfume of summer lilies. You need a minimalist approach to a winter garden, an appreciation of form and a sense of the dramatic – you need to see the merits of a stark line drawing over oils on canvas.

Why is this book different from other garden books? To begin with, it does not pretend to tell you how to garden in winter – there is more than enough already on double digging the cabbage patch and planting bulbs the right way up. Rather it is an attempt to explore what it is that can make the winter garden magical, unpacking the aesthetic thrill that goes with the sight of the ghostly white arcs of bramble or the flaming wands of dogwood, the bewitchment of a clean frame of yew hedging or the filigree of interlaced leafless branches, the shock of Titian tints in the spiral petals of a witch hazel or the royal purple velvet folds of a diminutive iris.

Very often we look but we do not see: we know that something is beautiful without appreciating why. This is an attempt to explain what it is that makes this configuration of planting, that setting, or this conjunction of structure the object of our fascination. We are trying to savour the nuances, to delineate the connotations and to realise the evocative. When something is beautiful and we are not sure why, it is because it has in some way inspired our imagination. We need to dissolve the nebula fogging our appreciation of things as 'romantic', 'pretty', 'dramatic' to see the shape of the forms beneath – what makes them romantic, pretty or dramatic.

Clive and I see things the same way. When we walk into a garden we will choose the same viewpoint, the same frame, the same focal point. Clive has the ability to capture these otherwise intangible qualities on film while I try to explain them in words. Most garden books are composed of pictures and purely practical information – how to, with what and when. They do not explain why that setting is beautiful or what makes it dramatic. They will stumble along with clichéd captions about 'a stunning setting', or 'a riot of colour'. On the other hand, brilliantly descriptive books have been written, mostly about the countryside, and sadly largely in the past, but these are unillustrated. What Clive and I have tried to do together, by marrying description to pictures is to elicit the aesthetics of the winter garden. It is about how to look.

Einstein once said that it was not the function of science to give the taste of the soup. This book does not pretend to science. It is about the taste of the soup.

The austerity of winter is revealed in the subtle colours and shapes of trees and shrubs (left), from the drooping branches of a weeping purple beech (*Fagus sylvatica* 'Purpurea 'Pendula'), and the fuzzy outlines of *Juniperus chinensis* 'Kuriwao Gold' to the stalwart Lilliputian army of *Hebe* 'Red Edge'.

STRUCTURE IN THE WINTER GARDEN

The basis for any garden in any season is always its structure but this is not necessarily a structure discernible in every season. A flower garden consisting almost entirely of bulbs in spring and herbaceous plants and annuals in the summer months may appear merely as earth borders in autumn and winter: it will derive its structure from the heights and colours of the plants, their disposition and arrangement only when they have grown. By contrast a winter garden, or a garden that is designed to look good winter and summer, must usually depend heavily on its architecture, or on using its planting in such a way that it becomes its own architecture, or a combination of both.

The distinction between man-made and natural, or architecture and planting, is not a particularly useful one in the context of gardens: all gardening in some way reflects human interference and is an attempt at the taming and trimming of nature. Yews do not normally grow as cones in parallel lines and water does not suddenly appear in two straight rills running alongside. Such a scheme uses planting as architecture in the best tradition of classic formality – symmetry and clean lines.

The yew allee (left) was created by the furniture designer John Makepeace and his wife for their house, also a residence for the students of their college at Parnham.

Sir Roy Strong's garden illustrates the use of planting as architecture. He has created a composition of frames within frames around a series of focal points along the same plane. The outermost frame is the opening between high beech hedges, preparatory to the change in level. Stone balls on plinths help to reinforce the classical symmetry of the design and are the means of executing a secondary theme of orbs, with the stone balls in the foreground balanced by the standard bay trees in the garden behind. The square which is thus formed by these orbs at its corners has the armillary sphere as its centrepoint, emphasised by the stone-flagged circle on which it stands.

But the subtlety of this design, based on visible spheres and circles and invisible lines of sight (the rectangle formed by taking the box and stone balls as corners), is merely the play within the play.

The more obvious elements of the primary design are the rectangular frames provided by the topiaried hedges. If the outer frame is, as we saw, the beech hedge, the inner frame is the stepped box hedge in the middle. Think how much more interesting this hedge is because it is stepped: if it were kept all at the level of the lowest step it would be tidy but predictable; if it were all the level of either of the two higher tiers it would render the foreground garden depressingly claustrophobic. The battlements function both as essence of the design and as a tease, allowing you to see just so much, then a little more and a little more. The stepping is also echoed by the further-

The importance of hanging a picture in a good frame cannot be overestimated as Sir Roy Strong knows. His Jubilee garden (below) leads into the Pierpoint Morgan rose garden beyond.
Stone steps, water and wrought iron (right) are both structure and content of the garden at Cornwell Manor.

most, higher hedge which is a nice touch. Sometimes a piece or two of statuary is essential to the design. Here, and from this angle, the figures at the far end are not essential to the design: it would be strong enough (forgive the pun, Sir Roy) without them.

The effect of the winter garden at Cornwell Manor has nothing to do with the structure of the planting and everything to do with the actual architecture, although it has to be said that it is made more glorious by the parkland beyond the gates, juxtaposing nature and husbandry (the parkland) with architecture and cultivation (the hard landscaping of the garden). It would make not a scrap of difference to the design of this garden in winter if the banks either side of the steps were plain grass, though clearly its effect when the trees were in leaf would be different.

What gives the structure of this garden its strength are the gates, their piers, and the steps. The pool provides a near and tranquil focal point, just as the gates provide a distant and delicate focal point. Having two focal points on the same plane, emphasised by the double set of piers and gates, makes, in effect, the same kind of statement that Sir Roy Strong's garden makes. And similarly, the rectangles of the steps, their horizontal lines and the vertical lines of the gates are both complemented and contrasted by the curves of the pool, the balls on the tops of the piers and the curves on the tops of the gates. Notice also that the steps have not been built in a straight run: they would have been very steep. Instead, blocks of steps have been terraced with wide flat plates in between. These not only slow the eye, they physically slow the walker as well, making both the visual effect and the physical effort leisurely, all taken at a civilised pace.

You may not have a manor set in rolling parkland, and you may not have the space to create a garden behind a garden as Sir Roy Strong has, but the lessons to be learnt from both these gardens can be applied to much smaller sites. For example, I have a friend with a very steeply-sloping garden. It is very narrow – only 10ft wide and 20ft long (3x6m) – in fact, it tapers almost to a point at the end. Rather than step outside and roll all the way down the garden, he has made as deep a patio as the contours permitted; and instead of

running a flight of steps down the remaining slope, he has terraced blocks of steps on a series of levels. Thus the same principle works as well for a small town house as for a manor house.

The judicious mix of architectural devices and planting to structure a garden for winter wear is illustrated by garden designer Anthony Noel's own small courtyard. His is a Victorian terraced house with a minute garden – but with restrained planting and the clever use of architectural detail, he has created a delicious combination which is both elegant and amusing. The wall facing the glazed doors is of old yellow-grey brick. Had it

been left as the brickworks intended, it would have made the tiny courtyard very dark, with an equally dark effect inside the house. So this wall and the rear wall of the house have been painted white which immediately lightens the area. To lend this corner some depth and indeed some length, Anthony has played tricks with perspective, using a double-arched trellis. He has clothed the wall with an evergreen climber, the ivy, *Hedera helix* 'Oro di Bogliasco', chosen for its colours: the green to echo the green painted trellis and the gold to give a sunny lift. Snow is a bonus adding white to white in the best of designer traditions.

The light and witty touch to a dark corner in Anthony Noel's London garden (above) is achieved with a mixture of architecture and planting.

The jaunty seaside air of Noel's pots carries through even into winter (above). The comical air of the lollipops of box and ornamental cabbage on thin twiggy stems defuses any suggestion of formal pomposity.

An enormous stone swagged urn would not be the first thing to enter most people's minds when designing in such a small space but here it works beautifully and the lollipop of standard box, in virtue of its small scale, is a witty reference to the trappings of 'ghastly good taste' and the sort of grand-scale gardens in which large urns and standard box usually find themselves. In fact, the same lark is repeated in a different mode, if you look carefully, with balls of box sprouting from ordinary terracotta flowerpots painted in jaunty seaside stripes of turquoise-blue and white. Even the roughly-brushed and dragged paintwork to the inside of the doors forms part of the overall composition – the sea blue-green, like a twist at the end of a short story, giving a spin to the more sedate and traditional greens supplied by nature and the trellis. It also melds inside with outside so the one flows into the other without any sense of disjunction. The whole picture provides a complete and definite structure for winter and a solid basis for summer when climbing roses will cover the house wall and alter the appearance of the courtyard with a lush fecundity.

Two wholly different approaches to structuring the winter garden with planting concern soft,

Winter makes a virtue of austerity and emphasises the rectilinearity of David Hicks' minimalist design (right). It succeeds in being both modern and classical at the same time and is indicative of a hard-edged, masculine approach. In contrast, the plump, woven tapestry of Rosemary Verey's knot garden (left) is soft and feminine. She has used box for the warp and weft of the knots and punctuated the corners with golden holly, *Ilex* x *altaclerensis* 'Golden King'.

low planting on the one hand, and high angular planting on the other. Both are geometric but whereas one, David Hicks' own garden, is rectangular – based on classic Euclidean geometry – the other, Rosemary Verey's own garden, describes parabolic curves and almost Mobius twists of modern geometry. Hicks uses trees in straight lines, at 90° angles; the horizontal chestnuts in the foreground framing the vertical allee beyond. The shape of the pool emphasises the perspective of the design and represents a miniature version of the entire scheme. The urns on plinths are almost superfluous in winter but serve to draw attention to the angles at the corners. As the surrounding land is flat, the straight lines of trees and paths make for an almost two-dimensional effect. This garden presents a formal, almost diagrammatic and very masculine approach to structure.

Rosemary Verey's knot garden, on the other hand, is soft, low growing and an essentially feminine structure using dwarf box. The effect is a plump, woven tapestry whose curves glide sensuously in and out and over each other. Both gardeners have used clipping to accentuate their effects: Hicks has taken the shotgun approach to his high horse chestnuts: Mrs Verey's effect looks as if it has – though of course it hasn't – been created with a pair of embroidery scissors. Both are classical in their own right, owing a great deal to early French styles but Hicks' structure is translated into a modern idiom whilst Mrs Verey's has a rococo feel. Like the urns in Hicks' garden, the sundial, from this viewpoint, is not essential to the composition but the tiers of clipped holly punctuate the corners of a three-dimensional creation contained within an overall rectangle.

Winter and Summer

This 16th century half-timbered house is surrounded by a two acre garden, using its planting to define its structure as much for summer as for winter. The main vista to the house is defined in both seasons by the straight lines of the allee or walk symmetrically planted on either side. The first thing to notice about this geometrical linear composition is that the overall effect in any of the four seasons is greatly enhanced by identical planting. Broad sweeps of the same material make bold statements. They make clean, unfussy lines which are what formal structure is all about. If you imagine the same long walk with bits of this and that, an oak here, an ash there, the odd poplar and dashes of different shrubs and perennials, the effect would be a total mess, however long and straight the grass walk is. We wouldn't even bother to write about it or photograph it.

In summer the geometry of identically-planted parallel lines is softened by the foliage of the limes (*Tilia platyphyllos* 'Rubra') and cushions – or a long bolster – of *Salvia purpurea* for the underplanting. The backdrop is insignificant except insofar as it is dense and dark behind the stems of the limes so the eye is not distracted by shafts of light or whatever might lie behind them. The overall effect is both handsome and luxuriant at the same time.

This juxtaposition of winter (right) and summer (below) at Wollerton Old Hall illustrates the virtues of the two seasons. The beech backdrop comes into its own in winter against the vertebrae of the limes: in summer these limes take all the glory.

Luxuriant planting to give a garden structure does not necessarily mean green planting. The corner garden at Wollerton enjoys a different kind of lushness in winter (left) after summer (above).

In winter, however, the limes take second place and that insignificant backdrop comes into its own for it is a glorious beech hedge of rich copper and auburn. Now the skeletal structure of the walk becomes visible and the limes punctuate its spine with vertical markers. The salvias still lie in cushions but they have given up their vibrant mauve spikes in preference for an elegant silver dressing of frost on what have become their grey-green leaves.

Not all structure has to be formal or geometric of course. The corner garden, bounded by a brick wall with a path to the gothic arched gate, achieves its structure by dense planting of the deep borders and against the wall on either side. Although this is dense, thick planting the effect is light and exuberant in summer. The wall is sprayed with the deep cream puffs of the rose, R. 'Lady Hillingdon' on one side and brushes of the deep green foliage of ceanothus on the other – a profusion of sky blues when in flower of course. The soft, frothy, limey yellow flowers of lady's mantle (*Alchemilla mollis*) and its downy leaves spill onto the gravel path on one corner, whilst the plumes of a deciduous fern sprout from the other.

Further along is a hydrangea, just in bud. In the winter picture we can see how its massive football flowerheads contribute to the generosity of the structure in even the most chilling conditions. It is relatively easy to plant a garden for the

23

effect of clean bone structure in winter or abundance in summer. It is more challenging to plant a garden for lush fecundity in summer and retain something of the same spirit in winter. This is where mixed planting – shrubs, perennials, evergreens, herbaceous plants and climbers – really comes into its own. The composition is achieved by the wild rush of the evergreen ceanothus high in the background, the balls of hydrangea heads, browned to a crisp, at mid-level and the drooping spread of the ground level planting.

In many ways this garden is an essay in how to leave well alone. Nothing illustrates the lesson better than the borders surrounding the gazebo. Deep, wide and stocked with traditional summer-flowering plants, it derives its summer structure from spires of deep blues and mauves of delphiniums, abundances of red and white valerian, shoots of downy grey lambs' lugs (*Stachys byzan-*

tina), clumps of crimson peony bowls and posies of roses. Everything soars upwards and spreads outwards, dressing the fretworked gothic lines of the gazebo with rainbow raiment.

The conventional thing to do would be to cut everything down for winter. Instead, the dying stalks and dwindling seed heads have been left in place as mementoes of summer fecundity, and also as blocks of wands, feathers, tassels, like piles of chaff on the threshing floor. It has the effect of bulking out the border, preserving a structure of forms and textures to be highlighted by the silver brush of a sharp frost. But it has another not so visible effect as well: its generosity in summer is a visual one; in winter it offers a refuge to unseen wildlife, providing cover and some warmth. For not only will birds feed on the remaining seed-heads, but the warmer ground will attract insects, food for birds more partial to a carnivorous diet.

The herbaceous borders at Wollerton are structured by the planting in summer (left) and by the architecture of the gazebo plus planting in winter (right).

Elegance and Eccentricity

The elegance of the little sunk garden at Gatacre Park is deceptive. The entrance down wide stone steps, framed by overhanging trees and symmetrical urns, directs the eye along a narrow oblong pool in the centre, planted on either side with the sentries of fastigiate Irish yew (*Taxus baccata* 'Fastigiata'). At the far end is an arch of common yew embellished with balls as if the uprights were stone piers. The area is only small – there are but three yews each side – and was once the site of an old potting shed and a collection of cold frames. It shows how, with very simple planting, it is possible to wholly transform a mundane site into a special, classically-elegant little garden that will look good all through the year.

So why is it deceptive? Well, if you think that the plain chic use of yew dictates the style of the whole of the garden at Gatacre you would be very much mistaken: fancy takes wing at Gatacre in the most delightfully eccentric collection of topiary creatures and domestic utensils and shapes as yet unknown to mathematics.

Here is a six-feet-high (1.8m) male teddy and a reclining teddy-ess; here is a fat teapot and a thin corkscrew; there is a toadstool and chess pawn, a swan and a peacock. Their creators are the late Sir Edward Thompson and Lady Thompson, whose father, the Reverend George l'Estrange Amphlett, was a renowned topiarist. He trained his daughters in the basic rules of topiary from an early age: grow from scratch and on no account use frames. Building on her education, Lady Thompson has made a menagerie, a batterie de cuisine and something she describes as 'an interesting shape with a bell on top'.

All the creatures in this garden began as self-sown seedlings: 'Yew doesn't grow everywhere', advises Lady Thompson, but contrary to popular assumptions it grows reasonably fast. After five years, at around five feet (1.5m) high and wide,

The charming conventional elegance of yew in the sunk garden at Gatacre Park (left) explodes into mirth when used for a fat teddy-ess (right).

Eat your heart out, Edward Lear. Here is the bird with the corkscrew neck (above) and male teddy, thin corkscrew and giant pawn (right).

they looked at them and thought of the shapes they might make, 'rather like that game you played as a child where you drew a squiggle and the other person had to make a shape out of it'. A powered trimmer is ideal: hand-clipping with shears may be traditional but is risky. The blades have to be very sharp or they will split the bark.

Thus does topiary offer a degree of excitement that goes beyond the merely ornamental or the Italianate. You can have a good deal of fun with topiary: a little loopy artistry that deserves respect. Next year's Turner Prize for art should go to the Gatacre Monster, a large, rotund animal sitting on the front lawn. Its summer plumage is yellow, turning a deep dark green with the first approach of winter. 'Bird thou never wert', says Lady Thompson, 'I'm sure I've no idea what sort of creature it is'.

Playing with Form

Hazelbury Manor is a large estate but the variety of treatments of form which it uses teaches all sorts of lessons about the handling of structure in winter, that could equally be used on a smaller scale.

The lime walk, for example, is a feature often associated with grander gardens but it is used here within a relatively small scale. It happens to be a part of a larger garden but that is irrelevant. An avenue of pleached limes would still make a handsome, if unusual, treatment for a small back garden.

But why is this structure so appealing? For a start, and most obviously, because of its symmetry and we are all programmed to appreciate symmetry. Second, because the clean lines of the verticals – the trunks of the limes – and the solid cuboid chunks of the yew hedging behind are sharply contrasted by the delicate spun sugar of the leafless branches. Candyfloss on a stick in winter becomes mopheads on broomhandles in

The lime walk at Hazelbury Manor (below) is all clean straight lines and symmetry, whereas the cushions of mixed conifers have a cosy, over-stuffed sofa appeal in complete contrast (right).

spring and summer: this is a structure for all seasons and a geometry amenable to smaller or larger spaces.

Moving on around the garden we find two structural treatments, so different one from the other that they deserve careful comparison. On the one hand we have a collection of conifers mixing the upright and the spreading, cones and mounds with long feathers. They have all become sufficiently established to grow into one another, the vertical surrounded by layers of horizontal skirts. It is an essay on the cramming together of different forms and the result is comfortable and cosy in the manner of an overstuffed sofa.

In total contrast is a mini Stonehenge: bare, odd, gaunt shapes of hard rock, some small, some larger, some leaning in one direction, some in another. At first sight, the stone circle and the mixed conifers have nothing whatever in common. One is plain, uncompromising, and the other soft and cushioned. But both are attempts to control space: the stones defining space and the

The stone circle (below) plays with concepts of space and matter. What is left out is as important as what is put in.

space in between, the conifers filling the space. Despite all their differences, the stones share something of the conifers' feel – not comfortable exactly, but the completion of a circle has a cosy quality of its own. It has a tranquillity that the busy shapes of the conifers do not possess.

Finally there is the laburnum tunnel – racemes of sunlight in spring and green all summer, but in winter you can see every bone in its body and the curvature of its spine along the metal supports. This structure, which as we know will be glorious in due season, offers in winter the delight of its tracery and the endless fascination of the tunnel form. In sum, Hazelbury in winter is all about using structures whose appeal lies in the manipulation of archetypal forms – phallic shapes and breast-like mounds, circles and tunnels. We may consciously choose our structures for good, solid horticultural reasons, dreams clothed in the civilised veneer of pretty flowers. But winter lays bare the roots of our choice and the springs of our unconscious.

The pretty tracery of the laburnum tunnel in winter (below) conceals its primaeval fascination.

Winter without Disguise

The very best historic houses are the lived-in sort. Not the ones where the family has been hived off to the west wing leaving the state rooms to the cold glitter of the chandeliers, a symbolic Berlin Wall of cordoned giltwood chairs, and tables heavy with porcelain that will never be used and crystal that will never again see vinous ruby. These are the Marie Celestes of the historic houses circuit: the life and heart has gone out of them.

Not so Chenies Manor, a red brick Tudor house with twisty chimneys and a battlemented tower. Charles I was brought here as prisoner of the Roundheads; Henry VIII was cuckolded here; and Elizabeth I signed Mary's death warrant here – but it remains a private family house, home to Col. and Mrs MacLeod Matthews. Mrs MacLeod Matthews rescued the garden from its surreal Victorian arrangement of vast drums of laurel and endless beds of asters, zinnias and marigolds attractive only to the frenzied imagination of overwrought divas warbling the lugubrious arias of High Victoriana. Now a series of rectangular gardens framed by trellis, yew and hornbeam hedging, punctuated by yew pyramids, like cones of green wool, are arrayed with tulips and forget-me-nots in spring and waves of cosmos and cleomes in high summer.

Whilst the garden is defined by paths and levels, low box hedging and topiary, the full impact of its structure is achieved by the skill of Mrs MacLeod Matthews' spring and summer plantsmanship. You can see how the elegant artistry of box hedging surrounding a statue and flanked by yew and box topiary is rendered even lighter and more delicate by the individual goblets of white tulips on straight green stems in late spring. No attempt is made to pack these spaces with planting in winter: the seasons must take their course and Cupid must stand naked in the snow without the benefit of breeches of ivy or jasmine jimjams.

Cupid has tulips for company in the spring at Chenies Manor (below) but must tough winter out without adornment, or indeed, dress (right).

This turf and gravel maze, based on a 16th century design for a penitential maze, is at its most impressive in winter when snow – or frost – defines its outline, lending another dimension to an otherwise flat piece of ground in the orchard. In the old days, a few laps covered minor misdemeanours: really naughty deeds required champion stamina, taking the gravel circuit on your knees. But for poor Catherine Howard, caught at Chenies in flagrante delicto with Thomas Culpeper (whose office, inappropriately, was Maker of the King's Bed), no penitential marathon would do. She was beheaded.

37

Apart from the fact that Cupid would spend all subsequent seasons from adolescence to old age smothered in greenery, the virtue of the plain approach to winter lies in its directness and honesty. There is no attempt to dissemble, to pretend that winter must be prettified for it to be endurable. This approach says that winter is bleak, is bare, but everything has its time and place.

Similarly, no attempt is made to disguise the dead and dying clumps of lady's mantle (*Alchemilla mollis*) spreading itself over the steps and paths behind cones of clipped box. The basic structure of symmetrical box and a central urn is made more interesting by intervals of steps and an arcade of pleached limes at the back: the picture is nevertheless severe and would be more so were it not for the aubergine leaves of bergenia. The scene looks especially severe in comparison with its spring and summer regalia. Who said life was fair? Who said winter was rich and vibrant? Of course winter is severe and bleak. That's what

winter is all about. And this garden is one that enjoys winter for its own sake.

Few gardens better illustrate the wisdom of leaving well alone for the winter. If you imagine a garden like this cluttered with winter pansies and ornamental cabbages in its borders and urns, you will appreciate that all its strength and drama would be lost. It derives most of its impact from its history and the appearance of its architecture. The empty urn, below, for example, stands in front of the windowless East wall of the house – windowless because at the time of the Plague it was believed that East winds alone could carry the malefic airs. The severity of brick unrelieved by casements is echoed by the severity of the empty urn, unrelieved in its turn by any pretension to pretty-pretty planting. Lone and leafless red roses surrounding the urn serve to emphasise the fact of winter death, their pathos itself derived from the fact that red roses are supposed to symbolise love. Eros opposes Thanatos. It is a very ancient theme.

Bergenia purpurascens clumps loosely about the stone steps in the sunk garden at Chenies (left), making an informal contrast to the clipped cones of box behind. The pathos of a few surviving roses around an empty urn (below) has a magical quality.

PLANTING IN THE WINTER GARDEN

You can build a winter garden entirely on the basis of structure and use very little planting to achieve a maximum effect. A rectangle of lawn, say, two parallel rills and an oblong pool at the end, the whole framed by walls, depends minimally on planting unless you are picky and count grass as plants. It's no good saying that ideally you would use a combination of structure and planting to achieve the perfect winter garden: some situations demand a predominance of one over the other. And of course, structure does not necessarily have to be formal: the loosest or wildest of arrangements still has a structure, and planting obviously is a major part of that.

When you are planning for winter think of yourself as a set designer. After all, unlike late spring and summer when the garden goes through as many scene changes as would keep an opera house's stage hands in employment, the winter stage is not going to change very rapidly. The catkins on a Garrya elliptica *may lengthen slowly, the hazels may put out their spirals of shredded orange peel, and the aconites may push their faces through the snow but the overall composition, in contrast to the frenzy of summer, is a static one.*

Just as a table is transformed by a white linen cloth, so ground structure will be transformed by a wash of snowdrops (left).

The cross-over between structure and planting means that it is very difficult to work on the basis of water-tight definitions of either. Take a group of hellebores and narcissi for example. Its own structure is that of a bursting bouquet. Multiply it times over in a circle around a piece of statuary or snaking through a lightly-wooded area and you have an overall structure. The grossest of definitions would push you to say that structure is about the overall shape – which may or may not be achieved with plants but could just as well be achieved with bricks and stone, whilst planting is about the combination and juxtaposition of colour and texture and form. But isn't that also what structure is about? Here we go again. Before we get in a hopeless tangle of definitions, let's look at some plants and their combinations. The mix of hellebore and narcissi is a delicious combination. The open circular sprays of dark green leaf to the hellebore (*Helleborus foetidus*) make a strong foil and contrast to the bright, sharp, upright lances of the daffodil's leaf, just as the mass of sprays of pale limey green flowers provides a canvas for the vivid yellow blotches of the daffodil. They aren't really blotches of course. What makes this such a clever combination in an artistic sense is that whilst both plants shoot up (as opposed to sprawling all over the ground), the flower heads of both plants point down. The hellebore's flowers droop in clusters: the trumpets of the daffodils point down or sideways and this effect is emphasised by the daffodil's sweeping recurved petals as if they are ready to bomb to the ground.

It's a whizzo idea for winter because the hellebore will be flowering long before the daffodils come through. When they do they add that extra fillip that signals the approach of spring. The hellebores look lovelier because their softness is highlighted by the yellow and the daffodils look lovelier because they are set in amongst a wave of pale green.

Daffodils are an amenable lot: they can be planted in little bunches or in Wordsworthian crowds and hosts. But just as some plants, like snowdrops, can be spread over large areas and it doesn't matter whether the land is flat or sloping, so there are others that look all the better for being set on a curvaceous contour. Perhaps the reason is that they are closer to their wild environment, but I'm not really sure. What I do know is that heather generally looks best on moors and mountainsides, wrapping the ground in a cloak of mauve mist, a colour as indefinable and as essential to its wearer as the blue of the Madonna's cloak to Italian Renaissance painting.

Heathers in gardens are a different matter. If the land is flat, no matter how many island beds you make sprouting with dwarf conifers and awash with sprawling juniper, and no matter how cleverly you mix their colours, the heathers will look as lifeless as the glazed eye of a dead fish on a marble slab.

This brilliant piece of planting is the work of designer John Brookes in his own garden, Denmans. The small delicate heads of the daffodil 'February Gold' spring up through the hellebore – a perk for the one and a foil for the other.

The only way they will look any good is coming down a steep slope, bounded if possible by dry-stone walling. Even the lowest of such walls will help – throwing the heather back, perhaps, into something more (or moor?) like its original environment.

The same holds good for dwarf conifers and sprawling conifers. Not a pretty sight on their own, and especially not on flat land where they generally form a lifeless, featureless mass. When they are mixed with an abundance of vigorous heathers on a gradient, they take on a vivacity they otherwise lacked. By using the densely packed and feathery varieties and interspersing

The horizontal bands of *Prunus serrula* (below) are all the more effective for being set against vertical foliage, while the gradient of the bank (right) gives this mix of heathers and conifers a vivacity they would lack on level ground.

ericas and callunas whose varying depth of colour matches the varying textures of the conifers, and by setting them all on a slope, you can create a sense of movement, a three-dimensional energy against which the flat island heather and conifer bed has all the dynamism of a waxwork.

When you are designing your winter stage set, therefore, place your props with care. Some things will need a backdrop, others won't. This *Prunus serrula* (left) needs a backdrop to show off its horizontal bands of deep mahogany. Of course it looks better for the sharp edge of frost defining the leafless branches, the arching evergreen of the cotoneaster behind and the play of lance and wire of the grasses at its foot. When all of those surrounding shapes are unified by the crackling glare of such Royal icing, the prunus bark's fire becomes the star of the show. But even when the frosts have gone, the mix of greens and muted browns will still throw this arch performer into the limelight.

Not so Mahonia. Because it has a strong architectural shape it is capable of standing alone, its sharp deep serrations and its fists of yellow fingers punching a pattern against the plainest of backgrounds. But although it looks fierce and strong enough to stand on its own, it is actually quite a friendly plant. In the photograph overleaf, it shares its space with the elegant oval gold and green foliage of elaeagnus (*Elaeagnus pungens* 'Maculata'). They have in common their colours and their elegance: they make a happy couple. Indeed, they could have shared their bed beneath

The glorious golden hands of mahonia are echoed in the golden variegation of *Elaeagnus pungens* 'Maculata' at its feet (left). Mixing hellebores with snowdrops (below and right) emphasises the modesty and shy nature of both plants.

and between them with a mass of winter aconites, whose sunshine faces and green ruffs would extend the same theme over the ground.

Good mixtures at ground level, that bring to life borders and corners that are waiting for the herbaceous plants of summer to erupt, are compositions of clumps of hellebore and snowdrop, which are wonderful in beds and borders as well as in wilder woodier settings. Hellebores do tend to get around a bit: they lead a rather racy life so the polite way of describing this example of their offspring is an *H. orientalis* hybrid. But its lovely bells of ivory splashed with pale green, of dusty rose and sugar pink look even better with their Lilliputian army escort of snowdrops, in bright white kit and green stripes.

Sheets and Blankets

Whether spread as one flat sheet over large areas of rough grass or crumpling together down the folds of a grassy bank, the mass planting of bulbs always looks wonderful. Some people are lucky enough to have exactly the sort of conditions that bulbs like best. At Benington Lordship, on the site of a Norman castle, seven acres of hillside defined by old walls and ruins and light woodland have made a perfect setting for a succession of flowers through the bleakest of months. Thousands of winter aconites (*Eranthis*) precede – just – thousands of snowdrops, but for a long period they flower together, yellow and white, winter's answer to buttercups and daisies. After them come a myriad scillas in a molten summer sky running down the banks, streaming through the trees to be shot through a little later on by the rays of sunshine daffodils. 'And all we did was to clear the ground a little', says their owner. 'I never planted a single bulb in my life.'

Perhaps they like the heavy clay soil. Certainly they like to be left alone. The most important thing from a bulb's point of view is the nourishment necessary to produce a lot of little bulblets. And if you chop down their foliage too soon in a mania for the immaculate instead of waiting for their untidy death, you will inhibit their capacity to naturalise. A minimum of six weeks after flowering is de rigeur: at Benington Lordship they do not cut the areas of long grass until July.

Allow bulbs the freedom to naturalise, as with these winter aconites and snowdrops (left) and daffodils and *Scilla bithynica* (right), and you will be rewarded by a better arrangement than any artifice could devise. Nature knows best.

When the countryside was a forest all its flowers were woodland plants. The natural setting for this cerulean shimmer of scillas heightens the aesthetic thrill they give us which no cultivated garden, however carefully tended, can ever hope to emulate.

Snowdrops and winter aconites are only one of many possible combinations. Snowdrops and chionodoxa, 'glory of the snow', in pale blue and sapphire blue stars, interspersed with the deep velvet blue of baby irises, are a really phenomenal combination. Palest pink to puce pink *Cyclamen coum* are a spread in themselves. At the Dower House, the cold wash of snowdrops moves into the warmth of pink cyclamens, and at the same time you will find clumps of egg yolk yellow crocus and the last of the winter aconites.

The combinations achievable with early bulbs are manifold but if you intend to go in for mass planting, encouraging them to naturalise, you might consider sticking to one species at a time. There is something incredibly attractive about a broad swathe of all the same thing, rather like the way in which you can dress a window. Masses and masses of a self-coloured cheap fabric, looped and swagged, can look far more elegant and voluptuous than standard amounts of even the most expensive patterned fabric. Even with all one species at a time there are lots of options: a mass of crocus varieties, say, pale blue and silver,

lavender blue and purple, gives a mix of shading but is held together as a design because they are all the same species within the same spectrum of colour. A slash of anemone stars, pink and blue and white, varies the colour but keeps within the species. And of course there's nothing like a host of golden daffodils, but haven't we heard that somewhere already?

But supposing you haven't a single bulb to your name and what you want are these sheets and blankets – in fact, all the bedlinen the world of bulbs and corms has to offer. Then of course you must buy them. But there are some, like snowdrops, which you are really best advised to buy 'in the green', that is, while they are still growing after flowering has finished. But check out your supplier and his sources carefully before buying. Like the beautiful, threatened bluebell, the pride of deciduous woodlands, many bulbs are stolen from the wild and sold to unscrupulous suppliers in the horticultural trade.

Snowdrops, wood anemones and winter aconites are all favoured targets for irresponsible digging. At the time of writing, whilst stealing

Cyclamen, winter aconites (*Eranthis*) and snowdrops around the base of a tree jolly up an otherwise dreary February day.

You wouldn't think it would work, puce and yellow, but it does. The combination of crocus and *Cyclamen coum* (below) achieves a balance of virtue in, first, the strength of both colours and, second, the fact that puce as a colour is actually based on a large amount of blue. Together with snowdrops (left) they make welcome the approach to The Dower House.

bulbs from the wild is of course an offence in many countries, it is not illegal to dig up wild bulbs, providing you either own the land or have the owner's permission. Thus you may see advertisements by people kindly offering to thin your bluebells or snowdrops, which as Miles King, Conservation Manager of Plantlife, says is 'an outrageous horticultural euphemism'. You might think you would have to be either philistine or incredibly stupid to be seduced by such advertisements, but numbers of people with the most honourable intentions towards their wild flowers are taken in every year so it is worth making the point. You should also be wary of advertisements offering these bulbs for sale 'in the green', unless they publish a name and address, because sometimes unscrupulously acquired bulbs are sold by P. O. Box numbers. Most large chains of garden centres operate a strict policy of selling only cultivated bulbs and require their suppliers to guarantee their sources. Buying bulbs from these outlets or from long-established reputable bulb growers is safest. Of course you can always grow bulbs yourself from seed – but be prepared to wait for up to six years before they produce a bulb of a decent size, which is what you want if they are to naturalise.

Wiles with Wands

Cambridge University acquired some thirty plus acres for its Botanic Garden in 1831. It is famed for its collection of trees, its scented garden, its many herbaceous plants arranged in families – and for its magnificent winter garden. You can visit this garden winter after winter and always find some new and novel combination of planting to inspire and delight you.

They have a way with stems in winter, these Cambridge botanists, which is nothing short of wizardry. Here it is as if all the fully paid-up members of the Magic Circle, including country members from Mars, have assembled a collection of their instruments of sorcery and by the simple production of their wands, before they even have time to mutter abracadabra, have brought about a magical transformation in an otherwise boring border. The brown twiglets of a less than fascinating hedge which backs the border become a weird and wonderful hairstyle by throwing into the

Even the very names of the plants in the Cambridge Botanic Garden have a wizardry about them: the hairstyle from hell (below) is an oryzopsis. The mad scramble of the centre shrub (right) is *Salix* 'Erythroflexuosa' and the ghostly brambles either side (*Rubus thibetanus*) add a spooky note to the scheme.

Gold and ruby flushes to the leaves of *Euonymus fortunei* 'Silver Queen' (left) make this a gem of a winter plant and the 'greenery-yallery' stems of *Cornus stolonifera* 'Flaviramea' bring out the euonymus' range of colours. The combination works well as an overall composition, the dense mounds of soft leaf forms complemented by the sharp upright shoots of the dogwood.

foreground an array of stems which combine with the hedge to produce the sort of transformation only jewels can effect in the hair of women of a certain age. The garnet fire of dogwood, (*Cornus alba* 'Kesselringii'), and the crystal white of bramble stems (*Rubus thibetanus*) are intricately woven and held together by the twisting gold branches of *Salix* 'Erythroflexuosa' into a wonderful winter parure that would turn any witch into a dazzling beauty.

Unexpected and break-the-rules colour combinations are seen in a mix of brazen orange witch hazel (*Hamamelis* x *intermedia* 'Jelena') with mauve heathers (*Erica erigena* 'Irish Dusk'). Of course,

one's grandmother always used to say that if you were red-headed you couldn't possibly wear pink: the colours would 'clash'. This is one of the rules flouted with verve by contemporary designers. The safe horticultural combination with orange is, of course, blue: by matching an underplanting of pretty mauve bells to the devil-may-care, raggle taggle gypsy flowers of the witch hazel, the Cambridge botanists have broken the mould, shunning the groves of academe in favour of excitement.

Working together leaf and stem and colour so that the one reflects or contrasts with the other is this brilliant play on greens (left). Shooting up

Brassy but classy. This witch hazel (*Hamamelis* x *intermedia* 'Jelena', right) is elegant in form, brazen in flower and almost more shocking for being surrounded by the respectable subdued mauve of the heathers (*Erica erigena* 'Irish Dusk').

Playing with fire: the red hot stems of *Cornus alba* 'Sibirica' against the gold glow of the conifer, *Chamaecyparis lawsoniana* 'Winston Churchill' (left) and the licks of *Cornus sanguinea* 'Winter Beauty' against more gold, this time *Elaeagnus pungens* 'Maculata' (right).

from the froth of *Euonymus fortunei* 'Silver Queen' are the yellowy greeny stems of *Cornus stolonifera* 'Flaviramea', all 'yallery greenery' as they used to say. They look like the whippy leafless wands of a weeping willow: imagine if you had those hanging over the cornus as well – what a treat. The curious thing about this combination is that it causes you to question the name of this variety of euonymus. The cream and green variegated leaf takes on a buttery hue: there is very little silver about it at all. The chameleon capacity of this shrub appears to have gone unremarked: perhaps it should be instantly renamed as *Euonymus* 'Precious Metals'. In fact this change in variegation is probably due to the maturity of the leaf. Younger foliage is always much cleaner and whiter, getting yellower with age. Nevertheless it remains true that if you grow this variety beside blue-flowering plants or plants with blue-green foliage it will look much less gold and far more silver and that if you grow it with yellower plants it will pick up – or perhaps your eye will pick out – the yellower variegation.

And as to special effects, there is a beautiful combination of great tufts of grasses (*Oryzopsis lessoniana*), fringed in gold and silver and bronze with their rich red lights echoed in the deep burgundy of the fleshy leaves of bergenia (*B.* 'Sunningdale'). In January, as the winter goes on, this apoplectic flush will suffuse almost the whole leaf. And the whilst the same colour is reiterated by the dogwood (*Cornus alba* 'Kesselringii') behind, the contrast in form and texture between leaf and stem makes the overall composition all the richer.

And finally, while we are on the subject of stems, there is little to match the punch of *Cornus sanguinea* 'Winter Beauty' whose mix of blond and lobster flails is given a depth and richness by setting it against a background of green and really gold foliage – in this case, *Elaeagnus pungens* 'Maculata'. On its own, or against a plain brick or stone wall, it would not look half as impressive. It is because it takes up something of the gold light behind it, that you are made aware of the potency of its coloration. And because the background is dense, it throws into relief the cross-hatching of its multiple stems, like a section through a bale of straw.

Good Grasses Guide

The strange thing about grasses is their propensity to alter their character depending on the company they keep. Separated from their fellows, they can become odd and gauche, uneasy in their surroundings. On the other hand, they can go the other way completely, turning into unimaginative complacent beings like plump suburban housewives. Gertrude Jekyll used spiky phormiums to punctuate the corners of herbaceous borders, the daggers of their sharp pointed upright leaves and the cutlasses of the bent leaves standing in relation to the soft and pretty plants of the rest of the border much as the juxtaposition of a Quentin Tarantino clip would appear besides the dramatisation of a romantic novel. This odd, occasional use of the plant out of context does it and the other plants a disservice, emphasising its savagery above its other qualities like a piece of gratuitous violence in a world of sweetness and light.

As a lesson in making a grass feel a part of an herbaceous border look at the picture below: an outrageous blonde wig exuberant between iron silver artemisia (*Artemisia* 'Powis Castle') and silver-green purple sage. The russet heads of the sedum (*S.* 'Herbstfreude', syn. 'Autumn Joy') are a deeper tone of the background asters (*Aster amellus* 'Pink Zenith'). How often asters are chopped after flowering is over: how wasteful of

The platinum blonde volcano of *Pennisetum alopecuroides* (presumably in translation: *Pennisetum* 'curious hair') is set off by the rust backdrop (below) of spent asters (*Aster amellus* 'Pink Zenith') and sedums (*Sedum* 'Herbstfreude', syn. 'Autumn Joy'). The balance of this composition (right) is achieved by punctuating the angles of a basic diamond shape with pampas on one side opposing the long wheat ears of miscanthus on the other, and by setting the extravagance of the pennisetum below the clean lines of the wrought iron stand behind. All the various spikes and stems and stalks are also balanced by the froth of the fill-in flower- and seedheads. A border like this deserves a pretty frost at least every other day.

Further along the magical border at The Old Vicarage (left) is a phormium whose savage swipes are cocooned by the soft fall of an overhanging miscanthus behind, browned off asters to the side and, in front, wisps of *Pennisetum alopecuroides* and woolly silver wands of *Artemisia* 'Powis Castle'.

the wonderful effect they make in the dead and desiccated state of winter and how mean to all the garden birds – they love aster seeds.

And yet, when you put together a collection of different grasses, they take on an altogether different appearance as the planting of this garden at The Old Vicarage shows. In part this is because they play on the same theme – they are all tufts and spikes of different kinds from the sharp spikes of the phormium to the cushioned plumes of the pampas (*Cortaderia selloana* 'Pumila') and the long wheat ears of the sheaf of miscanthus. In part it is because their colours, if not variations of the same colour, are technically complementary. All the grasses are based on blond, from the platinum blonde of *Pennisetum alopecuroides*, through the honey gold stems of the pampas to the ash blonde of the miscanthus. Even the shafts of the phormium are half gold.

The brilliance of this planting lies not just in putting them all together but in the felicitous use of the other plants to provide a rich foil of aubergine – like the sedums which pick up the aubergine of the adjacent phormium – and cinnamon of the spent asters in the background.

Phormiums, like yuccas, look foreign in the herbaceous border, a misplaced touch of exoticism transplanted into a gentler body and as soon rejected. On the other hand, as I said, it can all go the other way. The fat plumes of pampas grass standing on their own in a large garden of old and dignified beeches and traditional borders can look as ill-suited to their milieu as a well-fed, self-satisfied alderman at High Table in a university college, or the fashionable attire of the showy nouveau riche among the restrained classics of the county set.

The shapes of these plants are beautifully complementary as well as their colours. See how a miscanthus like a sheaf of golden wheat, arcs gracefully over at the top and how a phormium repeats the same action lower down the blade. The artemisia and the asters make a background frizz against which the vertical stems of the grass and the phormiums can be almost individually picked out. There is a harmony and balance to the whole composition both in the weighting of colour and the sorting of shapes: it is a harvest for the winter.

Clever Containment

Anthony Noel is a garden designer of enormous originality. His own garden is minute – no more than 17 feet by 40 feet (5x12m) at most, but that optimistically includes a 10ft (3m) brick path up the side of the house. He has transformed the seriously spatially-challenged into a gem, an objet de vertu, and at the same time nimbly dodged the dangers inherent in such creations, those of prissiness and preciosity, by bringing to his garden the quality of merriment. He disdains horticultural hauteur, encourages irony among the briony, mixes fete with fancy. The result is a tiny garden of style, wit and imagination. And it carries through into his winter potting and planting.

Winter containers can be divided into three groups: permanent planting; temporary planting and the container itself. Permanent planting is overall the least expensive but it can be the most boring: it boils down usually to looking at the same evergreen plant month after month, year after year.

There is another type of permanent planting in which the container is merely the vehicle for carrying the plant or for drawing attention to it. For example, the very formal severe lines of an agave are better seen in a raised position against a plain backdrop as they are in Noel's garden. This is a rare agave – *A. americana* 'Mediopicta', not at all your common green and yellow type, but glaucous grey and cream.

Noel's garden is a mix of formality and jollity. The formal and the elegant are seen in the pineapple of box with a necklace of ivy in a stone urn on a raised plinth. This type of container planting might in other hands have pretensions to pomposity but not sitting next to a stripy chair and a

Agave americana 'Mediopicta' and a helping of snow (below). Its shape, colouring and the fine detail of its teeth are all the better seen for its being potted on high in Anthony Noel's tiny town garden.

Mad, bad or beautiful, this collection of objects epitomises Anthony Noel's cheerful iconclasm (right). A pineapple of box in a stone urn might be found in any grand garden. But set it with the jollity of a stripy blue and white chair (a French 19th century conservatory chair, in fact) and the total hilarity of a puce painted pot, and the pomposity of the whole box-in-urn concept is revealed.

Daffodils (*Narcissus* 'Tête-à-Tête', left) look more charming because they have been planted in a shallow dish; and the cyclamen (below) may have been surprised by the sudden snow, but it really doesn't matter because their blue and white pots are even more riveting. By painting the chair a lurid turquoise, Noel draws our attention to its ludicrously ornate design.

puce pot which might or might not contain a pansy. It doesn't really matter: the lark is in the choice of colour.

Of course there are situations which demand this type of containment. The very formal garden, dependent for its elegance on classical structure and symmetry, may actually need two large urns either side of a flight of steps, each containing an identically-clipped pyramidal or spherical box, or standard bay trees. This type of treatment is part of the overall design of the garden – it would be lost without it.

Permanent container planting may include rhododendrons and azaleas and camellias that

must be potted in an acid soil. If your garden soil is not acid and you have always hankered for the glory of a great glossy-leaved camellia which will produce – for a limited run – its most perfectly sculptured blooms, then a very large container replete with acid soil is the answer. The trouble lies in its limited run for when it is not in flower, you may find it rather tedious although the camellia has the distinct advantage here in that its leaf is more attractive than the rhododendron's. Even more tedious in containers are the winter-flowering evergreens like skimmia. I had two large containers once which I planted, in a rush of enthusiasm for their winter flowers and scent,

with twin skimmias and sarcococcas. The latter bear scented, but insignificant, flowers and skimmia remains in bud for an awfully long time and spends an even longer time – all the rest of the year – without doing anything at all. I consigned them to a drab, shady part of the garden where they could get on with being drab and shady all together.

The trouble really lies in questions of space and continuity. If you have a large enough garden and readily available brute strength you can plant the largest of containers with permanent plants – trees, even – and move them about at will as they come into flower (always assuming that there is enough space for very large containers in their 'show' position – outside the back door or wherever). But even supposing you have the facilities you may still find this an unsatisfactory scenario: it does engender a sense of impermanence and a constantly changing landscape outside the front or back door does not have the same appeal as the regularity of seasonal changes to the same plant or plants.

Temporary container planting for winter is done in the full knowledge that you are going to discard the plants when they are done – like summer bedding – or find permanent homes for them in the garden. Winter pansies and ornamental brassicas come into the first category, heathers and certain shrubs into the second. Noel has used a perfectly charming terracotta dish (the fact that it is chipped adds to the charm) for a mass of very early daffodils which can be planted in the garden, after they have finished flowering, for the following year. There is also the halfway house: a central permanent plant, like a clipped box or dwarf conifer, surrounded by pansies in winter and petunias in summer with permanent ivies to spill over the sides, perhaps joined by trailing lobelia and helichrysum in summer.

Where the pots are small enough you can effect as much temporary planting as you like. Sometimes it's more temporary than you think. An ornamental puce brassica with its matching pot is another of Noel's creations and it's a very jolly and amusing little number. But ornamental cabbages are not wholly proof against a bitter winter: the outer leaves can go brown and die or sometimes the whole thing will give up com-

pletely in severe frost. Noel's miniature standard box, though, for all the frailty of its size and comic curve, will carry on regardless.

Temporary or permanent, Noel's recreation of elaborate Victorian trickery works wonderfully with pyramids of tough little muscari. Planted up a pole of chicken wire, filled with a mixture of earth and compost and covered in moss, they make an edifice which can be easily removed. Or they could be left in situ after flowering, tucked away in the shade somewhere to flower again next year. Like the rest of the garden, his pots are full of surprises.

Pink on pink and a good deal of brown show you can't fight against nature (below) but you can tamper with it, as this designer arrangement of muscari (right) shows.

ROMANCE IN THE WINTER GARDEN

Romance is a soluble notion. A thread of sunlight through black clouds overhanging a mining valley will transform a mean, bleak scene, catching a shimmer across the slate roofs of houses, firing the wheel at the pithead, playing with the chiaroscuro of the contours of slag heaps and hills. When the suture of sunlight dissolves, it leaves only the scarred and raw edges of a wound across the landscape.

Romance is immaterial but it uses material effects to call up its qualities unlike the purely conceptual beauty of, say, the elegance of a mathematical theorem. Antelope racing across the savannah is a physical image: its romance lies in its capacity to inspire ideas of freedom, wildness, nature unfettered by human interference. A romantic scene or image will evoke any of a number of disparate concepts – mystery, the unknown, death, new life, innocence, antiquity. It may be associated with sentiment or nostalgia but if it is heavily overlaid with these qualities it actually stops being romantic and becomes cloying and artificial. Romance is not a cliché, although the overuse of a romantic image, like the ubiquitous and promiscuous appearance of Monet's bridge on teatowels and diaries and chocolate boxes, can turn it into one. For a romantic image to have power – whether this image is conjured by painting or photograph, poetry or prose – it needs to have limited exposure: the freshness of the imagery in a phrase like 'the rosy-fingered dawn' becomes hackneyed if it is used a million times over to sell hand lotion or central heating.

Rosa 'Felicia' iced with frost (left) epitomises its beauty and bravery in the face of imminent death.

Not all romantic images are 'nice'. The image of the silent frozen battlefields behind barbed wire in 'All Quiet on the Western Front' or the aerial view of miles of white crosses marking the graves in Richard Attenborough's 'Oh What a Lovely War' are not 'nice' images but they are romantic. Romance can equally well be sinister, haunting, bleak, desolate, and despairing.

The romance of the winter garden runs the gamut between nice and nasty. And it depends for its effects a very great deal on the weather and the light. The combination of a hoar frost and a cold half-light makes this image of dying achillea very strong. Its limited colour range helps: just as the best photographic portraits of people are black and white and reveal the personality of the sitter without the distraction of colour, so frost focusses the form of the flowers with their narrow upright stalks and flat heads. It gives the overall shape of this composition an artistry it would not have had when the frost had melted and the midday sun left the plants in a dismaying mixture of dull brown and rancid greens. Notice, too, how the frost bulks out the foliage and defines each feathery curve and crinkle en masse so that the background throws the white heads and straight stems into relief. The romance of this image lies in its ability to convey the cold power and beauty of winter.

Whilst it is the architecture of nature which makes the romance of the achilleas, it is man-made architecture which makes the picture on the right romantic. The long, stone, arched colonnade framed by firs sits across a terrace overlooking a bank which falls away steeply. Classical architecture is inherently romantic in its elegance, simplicity, and the harmony of its proportions. 18th century architecture which sought to recreate that style is no less so. It is the more romantic under snow, tempered by the lack of colours – there is really only deep dark green and grey-white to play with – but also because it draws attention to the dignity, restraint and symmetry of the arcade. The romance of this image also lies in its allusion to man's power and control over nature: the manipulation of natural materials – hewed stone and yew hedging and the contouring of the landscape into level terraces and slopes – to make aesthetically pleasing geometric structures.

What the contrast between built or architectural romance and planted romance also shows is that romance is not necessarily culture-laden. The colonnade, of course, is evocative partly because it is a classically-derived structure but the achillea is an example of a much wider category of plants hit by winter. Mist and frost over a plant in the Himalayas would also produce the same impact.

The common-or-garden can be romantic too. A row of brick-built labourers' cottages with a humble timber picket fence to the front garden can be transformed by the luxury and gaiety of a cascade of brilliant pink roses in their frivolity of many-petalled can-can skirts. This is about the romance of innocence and courage, of brave blooms under

Romance can be built, for instance using architecture as in the Praeneste terrace at Rousham (below), or planted, as in the border of dying achillea at The Old Rectory (right).

Although it is the colour of the terracotta forcers (left) that makes this image work, it is their shape and the fact that they are old fashioned that makes the scene romantic. It is, however, the rose in frost and sunlight which gives this cottage scene (above) its romance.

frost, but the background of cottages also throws a rose-coloured backward glance at history. Life for an agricultural labourer – the context in which such cottages were built – was hard but not, as the rose shows, without its compensations.

This (left) might have been the back garden to the cottage above. It happens that it isn't but it doesn't matter. It is difficult to see a vegetable garden in winter as romantic unless there is something very specific about it like this little group of old-fashioned terracotta rhubarb forcers which impels you to look harder and suddenly see it differently. And this is exactly what the terracotta pots do. They are the only bit of bright colour in the scene and they are central so they immediately draw the eye. Having done so, they immediately induce a nostalgia for bygone methods of horticulture. Terracotta always looks very organic and the whole composition has a sort of Peter-Rabbit-hiding-in-the-watering-can appeal. But the final effect of these forcers is to make you look closely at the rest of the kitchen garden in winter and suddenly you see how really very pretty it is even in its most mundane aspects, like the rabbit fencing and the cordoned leafless, fruitless, fruit trees. Romance has its uses, even if it serves only to make us more perceptive and more susceptible to the aesthetic thrills of the commonplace.

The Mysterious

At 1,000 feet (330m) the Golfa almost qualifies as a mountain in Wales. A lot of the time the summit is obscured by mist which descends in swathes like a bale of silk unravelling over the counter. When that happens, it swaddles the top garden of The Dingle then follows its steep gradient down to levitate over the half acre pool at the bottom. The walk from top to bottom is a magical journey loosely bound by a thousand different shapes and textures. On the one hand you are compelled to linger over its own entrancement, but on the other, the vista at each turn drives you a little further on and down.

That shifting sense of realisation that you are about to enter an unknown world begins with the arch of *Garrya elliptica* at the end of the top, level lawn. Like the entrance to a grotto but lacking the tinsel artificiality of Christmas in department stores, the combination of long pale catkins and the dark drooping foliage of euphorbia shield the unknown, surrounding the very start of your journey with mystery which all the light, bright silver of the senecio cannot mask.

Once through the arch you are out of the normal world of lawns and flowerbeds and into the Narnia of strange forms and frozen landscapes. The broken ribs of fern plumes lie across the ground like a distraught ostrich, the untidy leaf-

The dark depths behind the *Garrya elliptica* 'James Roof' are made all the more tantalising by the garrya's long drooping catkins (left) while the whizzing, whirling branches of *Styrax japonicus* (right) will make your head spin.

Romance is not necessarily confined to the dark and misty. It can be brilliant too as *Prunus laurocerasus* 'Zabeliana', *Cornus alba* 'Elegantissima' and *Cornus stolonifera* 'Flaviramea' beside the pool at The Dingle (left) and the shock of bare branches of birch (*Betula utilis*) wrapped with *Hedera helix* 'Oro di Bogliasco' (syn. 'Goldheart') against the sky show.

less branches of a weeping purple beech (*Fagus sylvatica* 'Purpurea Pendula') hang down from its crown like the shocked mane of an ancient hag, while on two slender stems grow the whizzing, whirling branches of a *Styrax japonicus*, in frost a giant silver cobweb spun by some industrious Dervish. When you are dizzy with this play of forms, your eye attempts to grasp its colours but they are all evanescent muted half-tones – a semi-tone above white but below silver, blue-greens and gold-greens that resist fixing, hardly the stuff of glorious Technicolor but a millennium away from black and white. You might be caught in this landscape forever, turning around and around, unable to take a sighting in a sea of shifting shapes and indefinite colours. Romance has its uncertain side, too.

By the time you reach the pool, the rich and mellow aspects of romance have all returned. The great heat of the red and yellow dogwood stems and the pale cinnamon lengths of larch trunk are reflected in the water's depths via a bolt of sun-light, turning the ice blue of the sky into royal blue ripples of satin. With wonder at the sudden scene shift, exchanging the uncertainties of mist and unfamiliar shapes for a blue horizon defined by trees and the generous, comfortable mounds of red and gold, you turn and look up. The trajectory of a birch, its striations of peeling bark embossed by the green and gold clinging vestments of ivy, brings you face to face with the shock of a brilliant blue sky, the thrill travelling along every line of its branches and into your eyes. This is a winter garden which explores every aspect of romance.

The Operatic

This is Heale House. It is everything you could want in a romantic house: it is handsome and dignified and it comes with history – Charles II sheltered there in what he described as 'a hiding hole that was very convenient and safe' before he took ship for France. It has about it the straightforward elegance of architecture that needs no further frills. In consequence, a broad path of York stone between two rectangular lawns is without ornament. It leads directly up to the terrace outside the front, itself bounded by plain stone balustrading. Behind it and to the side lie the gardens and the River Avon.

When I first went to see this garden in winter Lady Anne Rasch was sceptical of its charms: 'The nerines are over and the hellebores are waiting to flower. It would be rather like being seen in my underclothes,' she said. 'Not that I look that fantastic in my overclothes.' She was, happily, quite wrong. She looked very good in her overclothes, and the garden, in its underclothes,

rimmed with frost and suffused with the watery shimmer of a barely-risen sun, was fit for a centrefold. Of course, we are not talking of the heavy corporeal characteristics of a garden but the ephemeral, intangible elements that help to define its mood.

It is as you look across the River Avon that marks the boundary between the garden itself and the surrounding land that you feel the first frisson of enchantment. This is the interface between the house and garden and its setting. If it is awkward in any way, if the juxtaposition of the cultivated with the husbanded is too sudden or severe, or if the one is not seen to flow from the other, there will be no romance and no marriage.

Along the eastern edge of the garden lies the balustraded boat terrace with stone steps designed by Harold Peto on either side, leading down to a platform by the river's edge. As the sun begins to strain through the muslin of early morning mists, the jetty recreates all the expectancy of a barque or a gondola. If I was filming La Traviata, I'd have Violetta standing at the

The broad stone-flagged walk up to the balustraded front of Heale House (left), originally laid out by Harold Peto and (right) his jetty on to the River Avon, appropriate for the most tragic of operas.

All the symbolism you could wish for, and especially for Violetta's death in La Traviata, in the pathos of this frosted musk rose and buds, its damaged outer petals shielding a purity within.

top of the steps, one pale hand resting on the balustrade, the other clutching a blood-stained handkerchief to her lips, as she rattles out her dying aria. The mists, which probably accounted for her tuberculosis in the first place, would be compulsory.

Before that scene, however, and in between spasms of hacking cough, Violetta might take a quiet walk under the pergolas that line the kitchen garden. The mown grass paths underfoot are soft and springy and lively but all about her are the images of decay, the more ironic as they were the fruits and vegetables that fed life. A few leaves cling to the dying vine but there is no way out: even the pretty wrought iron gates are barred and the river beyond, with the hope it offers of change and direction, is out of bounds. It is the end of the road.

Heale is clever because it uses the drama of its architecture – the house, the boat terrace, and the pergolas – without denying its natural setting. Gardens closed off from their landscapes, like the high yew-walled 'rooms' of the famous gardens at Hidcote, engender claustrophobia with over-cultivation. There is but one aspect there onto the surrounding hills and that through a wrought iron gate. The renfermé exclusion of great natural beauty, when it is there for the taking, turns a garden into a mere horticultural exercise.

The gardens of Heale are a different matter. A small, modest brick bridge with a coping of rough hewn stones and shaggy creeping plants leads from the lawns at the back of the house across the river and over to the fields on the other side. This is not the place for an avenue of smart pleached this or that. A row of pollarded willows, the native, natural tree for riverbanks here, with stems of burnt caramel, divides the river from the water meadows beyond but also unites the garden with its setting. The formal lawns have been transformed into a wild garden as the run-in to genuine agricultural land. You are as far removed from a chocolate box as you could ever get.

Between the house and the river is an evergreen hedge and, growing against it, a wall of hybrid musk roses, 'Penelope', 'Cornelia', 'Buff Beauty', 'Moonlight' and 'Felicia'. The rich jersey cream of their blooms and the carmine edge that makes a cupid's bow of the mouth of their petals are blotched with frost: the blooms and tiny buds droop down, and their outer petals curdle, brown and shrunk and desiccated. If this vignette of beauty freezing to death is not a romantic one, I do not know what is.

A delicate wrought iron gate bars the path out of the kitchen garden, cross-hatched with pergolas and dying vine, to the river and flood meadows beyond (right).

The Powerful

The solid face of romance was carved out at Rousham by William Kent, father of the English Landscape Movement. It rested on a pastoral idyll with vistas over parkland, lakes and streams carved out to yield the perfect view, tempered by the classic paraphernalia of temples on mounds, arcades, grottoes and statuary. Rousham bears all the stamp of Kent in this respect: reaching views across landscape and river to the eye-catching feature on the hill on the other side; languid pools in glades, stumbled across after a walk through the shrubbery; a Venus here and a temple there. They are romantic scenes in a predictable way: Kent's sensitivity and respect for the contours and textures of real landscape, as opposed to the French or Italianate imposition of artificial formality, epitomises a marriage between nature and art. But what gives Rousham's romance true grit is the fact that it is the hub of a working 1,700 acre farm.

The broad sweeps of land about the house are better appreciated in winter, unsoftened by the gentle flutter of leaves on the trees. Delineated only by bare hedgerows, the land looks cold and vast, guarded as huskies do their Alaskan territories, by the longhorn cattle Mr Cottrell-Dormer virtually saved from extinction – his is now the largest pedigree herd in the world. If you were setting out to design a bold winter landscape you could do worse than to use this for your template – but it has the added advantage that it is real. Of course the battlemented house, the pediments over the arch to the stable block, and the clock tower help enormously, and clearly at least one of the longhorns seems to believe she is as essential to romance as Marilyn Monroe was to the movies.

To the side of the house stands the rose parterre, an equally bold translation of, in this case, 17th century design. In winter it is all shape, the box diamonds surrounding box knuckle-dusters on a grand scale, giving you the feeling that you might be a visiting pygmy touring a Tudor garden. They emphasise the circular stone and conical roofed pigeon house built in 1685, and still inhabited.

For the boldest impression of all, that avoids

Longhorn cattle, not usually noted for their romantic image, nevertheless lend dignity and solidity to this view of Rousham House (right).

the pretty-pretty and really tackles the winter landscape, you must go to the terrace where Sheemaker's Dying Gladiator takes his last breath between the landscaped parkland and the house. This image is strong and uncompromising. It is all the better for the plainness of its surroundings, the dark depths of the firs beside it, the ribs of the stone balustrade behind it and the skeletal tree beyond. Kent made beautiful landscapes but none perhaps is quite so powerful as this. When he is acclaimed for arranging a marriage between nature and art, you must look not at Doric temples overlooking waterfalls framed by a woodland in leaf but at the severity and strength, the overall virility, of a match between landscape and classical sculpture.

The 17th century pigeon house forms the backdrop to the geometry of the knot garden under snow (left) while Sheemaker's Dying Gladiator (right) gives Kent's landscape drama and power.

The Witty

One of the most clever studies of different shades of the same colour is the painting The White Duck by Jean Baptiste Oudry and it is based on the most difficult colour of all, white. A white and very dead duck hangs against a whitewashed stone wall, its long neck resting against a white china bowl and its head lying on a white cloth. When the snow falls on this garden, it presents the same opportunity for playing with white – a white painted house in a garden under snow against a white sky. All the whites are, of course, different and what makes them so different are the different greens lying underneath, deep dark bottle green and glaucous blue-green, fresh ferny green and silvery steel green. The effect can be as romantic as a landscape that evokes a sense of mystery or innocence or freedom.

The romance of this garden and its surprises lie in four aspects: it plays with our ideas about colour, climates, countries and the themes of garden history. The colours it exploits are greens and whites; the climates and countries it conjures are Southern heat and the frozen North; and in between it weaves a few witty allusions to horticultural fashions.

Its summer manifestation is green, lush and Mediterranean, like the bowl of white nettle (*Lamium galeobdolon* 'Hermann's Pride') overhung by the long gold chains of office of an itea (*Itea ilicifolia*) and the flat green, flat-shaped exotic leaves

The magic of a heavy fall of snow transforms the otherwise lush landscape of this garden, playing with the effects of white on white (below).

of an Indian bean tree (*Catalpa bignonioides*). This is a chic summer dress, elegant and serene, perfect in every detail of its accessories and perfectly composed – very French. In winter it hugs its woollies of conifer and evergreen about itself – you are hardly aware of their existence at all in summer – and has swapped its french elegance for the comforting snow-shawls of Northern Europe. It has now a serenity of another kind.

The long border in summer is a lark: a witty way with Tudor conceits that cocks a snook at history and geography. At the end of the border is a mount, an allusion to the Elizabethan penchant for viewing the panorama of their estates. The double octagon of a square cut hedge of honeysuckle (*Lonicera*) surrounds a pygmy date palm

Mediterranean planting in summer (*Lamium galeobdolon* 'Hermann's Pride' in the bowl overhung by *Itea ilicifolia*, right) becomes the frozen north in winter (below).

(*Phoenix roebelenii*), an anachronism as far as the Elizabethan theme goes, but a witty reference to all Italianate gardens in general and the lemon pots at the Villa Lante in Lazio, Italy in particular. Who said romance couldn't be amusing?

By the time winter arrives, the date palm, along with its Italian connotations, has been safely tucked up in a heated greenhouse. Now the garden must rely totally on its framework and the play of green and white (weather permitting) to create an austere but nonetheless magical effect. You would be hard put to know where this garden is, so easily does it slide between geographical and political boundaries. Perhaps the greatest surprise is discovering that it is situated in a suburb of Oxford, a city of dreaming spires at its centre but of rather depressing late Victorian housing on its outskirts. If you didn't know this, even its front door would keep you guessing.

The Tudor feel to the green walk culminating in the mount dressed as a witty anachronism, with an exotic date palm (left), is obliterated by the sorcery of snow (right). Hydrangeas outside the front door (below).

WINTER PLANT DIRECTORY

I have tried to choose only those plants which are reliably hardy, and have specifically pointed out those that require protection. It would have been wonderful to begin my list with Acacia dealbata, *the gloriously-scented winter-flowering mimosa with its fluffy yellow pompoms, but it is really only half-hardy and had to be excluded for that reason.*

Almost every gardener will be able to show you, with pride, a plant that 'is not supposed to grow up/down/over here'. Whether his success is due to emerald-green fingers or to a sheltered micro-climate in that particular corner of his garden is not a tactful question to raise. But the prosperity of so many plants in apparently inhospitable climes means that you should take everything you hear about zones with a dish, rather than a pinch, of salt. The type of summer the plant enjoyed, the depth of root it established before winter and the water it contained at the point of frost all have a bearing on its hardiness. Nevertheless I have included the standard zone range for each plant, described in average annual minimum temperatures:

Zone 1: Below -45°C (-50°F)

Zone 2: -45°C (-50°F) to -40°C (-40°F)

Zone 3: -40°C (-40°F) to -34C° (-30°F)

Zone 4: -34°C (-30°F) to -29°C (-20°F)

Zone 5: -29°C (-20°F) to -23°C (-10°F)

Zone 6: -23°C (-10°F) to -18°C (0°F)

Zone 7: -18°C (0°F) to -12°C (10°F)

Zone 8: -12°C (10°F) to -7°C (20°F)

Zone 9: -7°C (20°F) to -1°C (30°F)

Zone 10: -1°C (30°F) to 4°C (40°F)

Zone 11: Above 4°C (40°F)

The frost-encrusted seed-heads of honesty (*Lunaria*) caught in golden winter sunlight.

ACER
Acer

Japanese maples are graceful trees in every season. Their traffic light autumn foliage is heart-stopping. Some forms do even better. In winter the young stems of *Acer palmatum* 'Sango-kaku' turn the most astonishing red, while your neighbours turn green. Not for nothing is it known as the coral bark maple. It looks fantastic against a frosted lawn.

Other acers for winter are those with textured and patterned bark. *Acer griseum* (paper bark maple) gives you all the glory of flaming foliage in the fall but also has a lovely peeling, warm, brown bark contrasting with its parchment skin underneath. They are slow growing – normally up to about 15 or 20ft (4.5-6m) but there is a splendid one in the Arnold Arboretum in Boston about 45ft (13.5m) high. Zone 5.

Snake bark maples have handsome, stripy bark: *A. pensylvanicum* has green striped with white and paler green, *A. p.* 'Erythrocladum' (shown above) has young stems of salmon and silver stripes (zones 4-7). The bark of *A. davidii* begins dark green and turns purplish as it ages (zone 7). And *A. grosseri hersii* has a deliciously cool bark that looks as if it has been given a faux marbre treatment (zone 7).

ADONIS
Adonis

With their late winter flowers like open buttercups with a frilly edge and a satin finish, and dark green ferny foliage, these plants form clumps from fibrous roots and come in pink, white or yellow. They are most effective as a bolt of one colour. Choose from *A. amurensis* which grows about 6in (15cm) high; *A. a.* 'Flore Pleno' which is the double form, yellow with a green eye; or *A. a.* 'Fukujukai' shown above.

A. brevistyla has a simple white buttercup flower and golden anthers at its throat – the leaf is more finely cut; *A. vernalis* is slightly later flowering and has longer daisy-like petals.

It disappears below ground entirely by mid July so you must remember where it is. Zones 4-7.

AJUGA
Bugle

Ajuga reptans is the common bugle plant. Although its spikes of blue flowers do not appear until the spring, its shiny purple or deep bronze foliage makes it a good choice for winter cover. It is low growing, about 6in (15cm), and creeping. It looks good with clumps of ophiopogon which has long tufts of black grass leaves, or between the higher dark wine flowers of *Helleborus orientalis*. Allow little bunches of bulbs to push through, like the striped squill, *Puschkinia scilloides* with its white bells, or the dog's tooth violet in palest yellow. The green and bronze tortoiseshell pattern of its leaves goes well with the bronze sheen of the ajuga.

A. reptans 'Braunherz' is purple-bronze; *A. r.* 'Atropurpurea' is a dark green, purplish bronze; *A. r.* 'Catlin's Giant' (shown above) is a large, purple form and *A. r.* 'Burgundy Glow' is dark reddish, bronze and cream. Zones 4-8.

ANEMONE
Windflower
Its common name – the windflower – is in itself enough to make you want this in your garden. It comes from the Greek, anemos, meaning wind. The most common winter species is *A. blanda* (shown above), which sounds odd because it is not in the least bit bland until you realise that *blandus -a -um* means charming so that makes it quite all right. It comes not only in white but also pink, blue, mauve and even red which is a bit bossy for a small, simple flower.

The simplest little stars of white with yellow centres stand upright among bright green leaves braving the frosts at the end of winter. *A. b.* 'White Splendour' is the best white form, 2-4in (5-10cm) high. *A. b.* 'Ingramii' is sky blue with a yellow eye. It is a tough little plant, fully hardy and a joy not to be missed.

A. nemorosa is the wood anemone, masses of white flowers and yellow stamens, but later in flower. Plant under trees – like *A. blanda* it loves semi shade. Cultivars include the double white 'Alba Plena' and the pale blue 'Robinsoniana' both of which look good in a more cultivated garden setting. Zones 7-9.

ARBUTUS
Strawberry tree
An evergreen tree, of spreading habit, not overly impressive in terms of its shape, but good for its flowers and fruit and, in some cases, bark. *A. unendo* (*unendo* means I eat it once – and, presumably, never again) has look-alike strawberry fruits which are tempting but tasteless. Delightfully, it bears flowers and fruits at the same time because its white pendant flowers appear from autumn to winter at the same time as the previous season's fruits begin to ripen.

A. unendo rubra has pinkish red flowers. *A.* x *andrachnoides* is the more interesting. Its white flowers start opening in December in little bunches alongside its red fruits but it also has the added attraction of cinnamon stick peeling bark. Like *unendo* its leaves are a deep glossy green. Slow growing but worthwhile and tolerant of lime and coastal conditions. It is extremely hardy. A friend had one which prospered magnificently in an area famed for its bone-chilling winters. Zone 8.

ARTEMISIA
Wormwood
With such a pretty botanical name and such an off-putting common one, you would be right to expect a few more contradictions in this shrub. For a start those species which are described as evergreen (and not all are) are, in fact, ever silver. And this is why it should be highly prized in the winter garden although how long it will hang on to its silver finery is a function of the climate.

A. arborescens is not reliably hardy but *A. a.* 'Faith Raven' was collected in the mountains of Crete and is frost-hardy with fine cut silver-white foliage. Although it is classed as an upright shrub it will tend to flop about. Laid back is how you would describe it if it were a person. By contrast *A.* 'Powis Castle' (shown above) is also frost-hardy and far more together, assembling its ferny foliage in a clump like some silver-green cumulus cloud. They all have a lovely dry aromatic scent when crushed. Zones 5-8.

BAMBOO
Bamboo
Bamboos have a typically tranquil appearance, they are evergreen and frost hardy so you can keep your hair on. My bamboo runs the length of an 8ft (2.4m) long wall and looks green and spruce all year. However I doubt there is much more than one square meal in it for a panda.

Pretty bamboos include: *Phyllostachys aurea*, the fishpole or golden bamboo with grooved stems and mid green leaves; *P. bambusoides*, timber bamboo, with shiny, broader green leaves and bristly leaf sheaths; *P. flexuosa*, zigzag bamboo, with slender, noticeably zigzag stems that go black as they age; *P. nigra* with stems that go black as early as their second year.

Many other bamboos are fuller and bushier than phyllostachys, such as the green and white striped *Pleioblastus variegatus* on zigzag canes and *Fargesia nitida* (shown above) on stout golden canes.

All these reach an eventual height of 20-25ft (6-7.5m). The crucial thing is that they needn't because you can simply keep cutting it back. I trim mine regularly top and sides just as if it were a hedge. And it's perfectly happy in the shade. Zone 7.

BERGENIA
Bergenia
I used to think these were the ugliest plants in the world with their great round fleshy maroon leaves like an embarrassed giant cabbage. In my childhood they grew in two large clumps at one end of the long walled border. I realise now that this early repugnance denoted a fascination with the things, and whilst I now in fact like them I don't believe they are suitable for every garden. They are best for large gardens: when described as clump-forming, read big-clump-forming. They do look good at the end of a long border; they also look very good near water.

B. cordifolia 'Purpurea' is evergreen, with dark, dark green soup-plate leaves flushed purple at the edges and bears clumps of rose-pink bellflowers on red stems from late winter into spring. *B. x schmidtii* has a frillier edge to its leaves, flowers – again rose pink– in late January; whereas *B. crassifolia* (shown above) flowers a little later in mauve-pink rather than rose, but has leaves that turn a rich mahogany in winter. They all look wonderful in a hoar frost. Zones 4-8.

BETULA
Birch
The most delightful of trees in any season but winter emphasises its particular grace. A long elegant trunk and the delicate tracery of its leafless branches hung with a lace of frost make it a jewel in the winter garden. *B. utilis* var. *jacquemontii* (shown above) is the western cultivated form of the Himalayan birch. It has a smooth white bark to its trunk, a polished whitewash that demands to be lovingly stroked. It will appreciate a wash and brush up with a soft scrubbing brush and a little detergent in the water: it will kill off any algae and look all the better for it.

This form will grow to 30ft (9m) with a spread of 20ft (6m) and puts up with dry conditions. Another, perhaps even lovelier form, *B. utilis* var. *jacquemontii* 'Silver Shadow', has dazzling white stems and dark drooping leaves. *B. albosinensis*, with the same height and spread, has copper-orange stems which peel beautifully. The bark of *B. nigra* 'Heritage' peels in thin layers pinkish brown to white urging you to pick at it like a bad suntan. *B. pendula* 'Dalecarlica', the Swedish birch, has a slim white trunk and tiers of pendent foliage like lace drapes. It is, however, lanky rather than elegant. Zone 6.

BUXUS
Box or boxwood

This most excellent genus of evergreen shrubs and trees is indispensable in the winter garden. I regard box as a sculptural material: it makes wonderful low hedges for edging because it takes regular trimming without complaint, it makes lollipops or mopheads on narrow stems for pots or more dignified pyramids for urns. You can make domes or mounds or balls of varying sizes to punctuate long hedging or edging and you can practise your artistic skills on it for topiary.

B. sempervirens 'Handsworthiensis' is dense and vigorous and grows to about 10ft (3m), making it ideal for hedging and grand-scale topiary work. At the other extreme is *B. microphylla* 'Green Pillow' which makes dense dwarf domes of oval dark green leaves. In between is *B. sempervirens* 'Suffruticosa' which will grow to about 2¹/₂ft (.75m) high if you want it to, but will happily tolerate trimming down to 6in (15cm) for edging. *B. s.* 'Elegantissima' (shown above) is dwarf and domed – its leaves have cream margins. Zones 7-8.

CALLICARPA BODINIERI
Callicarpa bodinieri

When it has lost its pale green and pale bronze leaves, *Callicarpa bodinieri* var. *giraldii* (shown above), a Chinese many-stemmed shrub, is garnished with clusters of berries from puce to pale mauve or deep violet. It has an eventual height and spread of about 6ft (1.8m) and in summertime has tiny lilac flowers.

C. bodinieri var. *giraldii* 'Profusion' is well named. The berries are lavender rather than puce and although it takes time to get going, it prefers a promiscuous lifestyle – plant several together for cross-fertilization – it will reward you with all berries bright and beautiful. Zones 6-9.

CALLUNA VULGARIS
Scottish heather or ling

One of the three genera that comprise heathers which in general, Calluna in particular, require an acid soil. Calluna has only one species, *C. vulgaris*, which used to be dried off and used in a bunch for brooms. Unlike ericas which flower in winter or summer (and some of which also flower in spring and autumn), callunas flower from mid summer to late autumn.

Nevertheless their foliage makes them essential for winter gardens. *C. v.* 'Wickwar Flame' (shown above) is the arsonist's choice turning bright red in winter while *C. v.* 'Golden Carpet' is for the impressionist-arsonist, flaring orange and red. *C. v.* 'Foxii Nana' makes a small green dome in winter; 'Golden Feather' has wands of limey gold and 'Boskoop' is a lovely mix of tawny, red and white. Zone 5.

CAMELLIA
Camellia

Glossy, evergreen leaves and lustrous blooms which in their size and colour betray a sensuousness that the often disciplined sculptural form of its petals denies, the camellia is one of the most wonderful winter shrubs. It needs an acid soil.

Camellia flowers enjoy a range of styles: some, as I said, are very disciplined and proper, some freer spirits. Some appear to be understudies for other flower forms: the formal double reminds one of certain kinds of dahlia. The peony, anemone and rose forms all justify their classification.

Winter bloomers include *C. hiemalis* with cups single, semi or irregular double in pink white or red. Fragrant and bushy, growing to 6-10ft (2-3m), it is good for hedges. *C. vernalis* is a fast grower to about 10ft (3m). Bright green leaves and, in late winter, flat or cup shaped single white, pink or red flowers. *C. sasanqua* 'Narumigata' throws out scented blooms, white tipped pale pink, but needs shelter from frost. *C. s.* 'Crimson King' (shown above) has rich crimson blooms.

All camellias benefit from protection. An east wind or harsh early morning sun after frost can burn the petals badly. Zones 7-9.

CAREX PENDULA
Pendulous sedge

Unrivalled for its pretty, delicate, long thin 'catkins' in summer and fine narrow leaves that arch over, this is an evergreen sedge that looks graceful anywhere. It grows to about 3ft (1m) high with a tuft diameter of about 1ft (30cm).

Other carex species to try include *C.* 'Frosted Curls' (shown above) which has narrow, dark bronze-green leaves with the added attraction of looking as if they are under white frost, even when there isn't any. If you want to make a winter garden that looks really wintry, plant this all over the place. (It still looks like this in summer). *C. hachijoensis* 'Evergold' has shiny, narrow leaves striped green and yellow, and *C. testacea* yellow and green stripes that go bronze and green in winter. Zones 6-9.

CEDRUS
Cedar

From 80ft (24m) down to 3ft (1m), these conifers offer a range of possibilities geared to garden size. The best are the biggest and of those are two of the most beautiful trees in the world. The Atlantic or Atlas cedar is a dark green but *Cedrus libani* ssp. *atlantica* Glauca Group (shown above) is a most beautiful colour, a bluey grey that looks like silver-dipped blue slate. It begins fairly conical and as it grows older it throws out graceful, sweeping branches. It can get to 80ft (24m) with a spread of 15-30ft (4.5-9m), but slowly. *C. l.* ssp. *atlantica* 'Glauca Pendula' is a lovely version, smaller – to about 30ft (9m) high, with drooping branches. Zone 9.

The other most beautiful is the cedar of Lebanon (*C. libani*), which in shape and majesty outrivals the Atlas cedar. With many branches carrying its dark green foliage in flattened, arching tiers, it is a triumph of the Arch Designer's creation. It can attain the same height as the Atlas but has a much greater spread – up to 50ft (15m). Zone 9.

CHAENOMELES

Japonica, Japanese quince
A lovely shrub, useful for growing against walls, pretty flowers often on bare branches and fruits which make the most delicious jelly, especially good with cold meats. A *much* nicer alternative to pyracantha or cotoneaster.

C. speciosa will often flower on and off through the year even in late autumn and winter especially if grown against a warm, sunny wall. *C. s.* 'Moerloosei' makes a bushy shrub of 10ft (3m) in height and spread or can be trained against a wall. Lovely apple blossom, salmon-pink and white flowers from early spring.

C. x superba 'Rowallane' has bigger, waxy, scarlet flowers and glossy dark green leaves. Some books will tell you that it has a height and spread of 6ft (1.8m) but I have seen the original at Rowallane, Co. Down, N. Ireland, now belonging to The National Trust, where it has spread to cover most of the high stone wall and arch that forms the entrance to the Wall Garden. Zones 5-9.

CHIMONANTHUS PRAECOX

Wintersweet
One of the dearest, simplest, old-fashioned winter-flowering things, wintersweet smells like nectar. And although its pale gold petals shielding the inside petals, veined in maroon-purple, cheer the heart by their colour on leafless branches, this is a plant with pathos. It is something to do with the way the petals droop down, huddled in bunches – the Little Match Girl of winter. Its spirit has nothing in common with witch hazel blossom, a jolly, blowsy tangle of a carefree strumpet with a heart of gold.

A spray of wintersweet in a jar will scent an entire room, if it is warm, after a few hours. I was given one of these lovely plants two years ago to plant against the south-facing wall by my front door – it needs protection because a severe frost can hurt its flowers – with the injunction 'be patient'. I am but it will be another three years or so before it flowers.

C. praecox 'Luteus' has bigger flowers with gold inner petals and a better scent, and grows to 10ft (3m). In leaf it is boring, but I have a succession of climbers intertwined with it – white wisteria and white clematis – for distraction. Zones 7-9.

CHIONODOXA

Glory of the snow
And it is. Little pale or lilac-blue wax stars with six long, separated petals, a white eye and yellow stamens peep through the rush of their longer green leaves at the end of winter as if, with their startled faces – it's the white that gives them that look – they are saying, 'Surprise, surprise! Spring is nearly here'. You must plant them in clumps so they can have a little giggle between themselves. Don't even think of straight rows.

C. luciliae (syn *C. gigantea*) is only 2-4in (5-10cm) high, but the flowerheads themselves are giant in proportion and are a bright pale cerulean blue. *C. forbesii* can be twice as high, in a deeper lavender-blue, whilst *C. sardensis* are virtually gentian and without the white eye. *C. forbesii* 'Pink Giant' makes them sound revolting. In reality they are white at their centre moving to a flush of palest apple blossom pink to the last third of the petal. I find it more difficult to accommodate pink in the late winter garden. If I did, I would have to reorganise the crocuses and go for pale violet, with the deep purple, open flowers of *Bulbocodium vernum* and pale pink and white flushed cyclamen. Zone 4.

CHOISYA

Mexican orange blossom

Nothing replaces real orange blossom, or lemon blossom for that matter, but unless you enjoy a warm climate or conservatory you must forget the real thing. Choisya's evergreen foliage is nothing like an orange tree. It offers bouquets of open, shiny, rounded leaves made up of three well separated leaflets and, when in flower, clusters of pretty white stars that smell sweetly. There is now a yellow foliage form, *C. t.* 'Sundance' but I prefer the traditional variety for its good strong colour in winter. In any case, 'Sundance' loses its sick-making hues if grown in semi-shade and reverts to green. *C.* 'Aztec Pearl', as you might suspect, begins with pink buds opening whiter.

Choisya flowers in late spring, again in the autumn and sometimes in winter. People tell you that they are not fully frost hardy but in Oxford, which has frosts that would make you breathless with incredulity, they do remarkably well. Height around 6ft (1.8m) (higher in Oxford, I swear), spread about 5ft (1.5m). 'Sundance' is smaller and a zone or two less hardy. Zones 7-9.

CLEMATIS

Old man's beard, traveller's joy

It's because so many clematis seed heads go into a pale whorling, whirling tangle that it is known as old man's beard and as for traveller's joy, it's either the scramble of climbing flowers or the drift of white whiskers. Nothing is lovelier early on a winter's morning when the light catches cobwebs slung between these whirls, in necklaces of frost. And for this reason alone, it is worth keeping the seedheads in your winter garden (especially *C. tangutica* and *C. orientalis*).

Some species are winter flowering and evergreen, however. *C. armandii* needs a sheltered site but is frost hardy and flowers from January. With big, long leaves in a heavy green, it bears copious white star cups, delicately scented. *C. a.* 'Apple Blossom' has a pale flush of eponymous sepals. Height and spread to about 16ft (5m). In milder climes, *C. cirrhosa*, though it sounds as if it has spent its life in hard drink, has pretty, delicate cream bells, freckled deep red inside, when there is no frost about. *C. c.* var. *balearica* is shown above. Zones 7-9.

CORNUS

Dogwood

I am devoted to this family, especially *C. nuttallii*, for its white flower bracts in late spring. Impressive winter species are prized for their leafless stems in a mass of thin red, orange or yellow licks. *C. alba* has dark red stems, *C. a.* 'Sibirica' (shown above, syn. 'Atrosanguinea' and 'Westonbirt') is pillar box red, *C. a.* 'Kesselringii' has deep purple stems and is especially good beside a ghostly white rubus (zones 3-9). *Cornus sanguinea* 'Winter Beauty' glows gold in autumn leaf until all that is left are red stems, orange at their base and pink at their tips (zones 5-6). *C. stolonifera* 'Flaviramea' has yellowy green stems (zones 3-8). These look especially good beside water.

There is also a delightful cornus for winter flowering. *C. mas*, the cornelian cherry, is prolific with bright acid yellow buds that appear in autumn and burst in winter, smothering leafless branches so that you might hardly realise they were leafless. It grows to about 10ft (3m), a good size for a small garden. *C. mas* 'Variegata' in due season has a dark green leaf with a wide band of pale cream to its edge (zones 4-8).

CORTADERIA

Pampas grass

A mature, massive clump of pampas grass, with its elegant arching habit looks more striking in winter when there aren't the distractions of lush rampant foliage of summer. It grows to about 10ft (3m) high with a spread of about 5ft (1.5m) and the plumes are silver-cream. It is tough as old boots. In a very, very cold winter it will get browned off – the old foliage does this as a matter of course anyway. You are supposed to deal with this by setting fire to it in spring. I did this years ago with an ancient tatty clump and everyone thought I had finally gone completely mad. It does come back, though, believe me.

Pampas grass can look oddly exotic in some gardens, out of kilter with very traditional planting. Be careful where you put it. Be just as careful how you handle it: the leaves can cut your hands horribly. *C. selloana* 'Pumila' lasts well. *C. s.* 'Albolineata' has a white edge to its leaf and is slightly more tender. Zones 8-10.

CORYLOPSIS

Fragrant winterhazel

This plant drops masses of little funnels of delicately-scented, pale yellow flowers which at a distance look like an exuberant pointilliste representation of the herald of spring. When young leaves do appear they are bronze, turning bright green. Corylopsis makes a good backdrop shrub, but you wouldn't really want to turn whole beds over to it.

The flowers may be killed by heavy frosts but in mild winters, flowering should begin in February. It really needs an acid soil. *C. pauciflora* has a height and spread to about 5ft (1.5m). *C. glabrescens* is a little later flowering, dropping its flowers like catkins. Its overall shape is like a wheatsheaf, at least twice as big as *C. pauciflora*. *C. sinensis* var. *sinensis* 'Spring Purple', with a height and spread of 12ft (3.6m), bears plum coloured young leaves until they age, when they turn bright green on the top with a blue green underside. Zones 6-8.

CORYLUS

Hazel

The true hazel bears long yellow catkins in late winter and, preferably, nuts in autumn. *C. maxima* 'Purpurea' will grow to 20ft (6m) and a little over half that in spread. However, hazels can be coppiced. If you do this every two or three years you will have lovely fresh stems from the base and a smaller fresher tree. It has purpley catkins with yellow anthers on bare branches in February; it has wonderful purple-bronze leaves when in foliage; and it has filberts in autumn. What more could you ask for?

Well, some people prefer the agitated Quasimodo look of *C. avellana* 'Contorta' popularly known as the corkscrew hazel or Harry Lauder's walking stick, its twisty stems making mad, spiralling scribbles against the sky. This tree makes me feel unhappy and uncomfortable but doubtless this is a figment of an overwrought imagination. Certainly it will look quite odd in a garden where everything else is straight or arching. It grows about 6-8ft (1.8-2.4m) high and as wide. Zones 5-8.

COTONEASTER
Cotoneaster

Cotoneasters are prolific berriers – scarlet, orange, yellow – but finding one whose fruits will persist well into winter is not easy, not least because birds go mad for them. Not all are evergreen, either. *C. frigidus* 'Cornubia' has a good spread of 10ft (3m) and will grow into a small tree of 15ft (4.5m) if you let it. It has masses of scarlet berries from autumn through winter but it is only semi-evergreen (zones 7-8). *C. simonsii* makes a good semi-evergreen hedge with glossy leaves and scarlet berries. Height to 8ft (2.4m) and spread to 6ft (1.8m). Zones 6-9.

Arching types include *C. salicifolius* 'Exburyensis' and *C. s.* 'Rothschildianus', very graceful with its pale gold berries hanging in racemes. Height and spread to 10ft (3m). Zones 6-8.

C. horizontalis is, naturally, good against walls with a height to just under 3ft (1m) and a spread of 5ft (1.5m). It has scarlet berries and dark leaves along herringbone branches.

CROCUS
Crocus

There are enough species to keep your garden fully crocussed from autumn to late spring. Artistically adaptable, they can be planted as drifts over lawns or hillsides, massed in borders or arranged in little posies under a tree.

You can start off in autumn with *Crocus speciosus* 'Conqueror', cups of summer sky, veined in lavender, a golden throat and saffron stigmata. If you want real saffron, however, you must use *C. sativus* for these saucers of purple contain the bright red stigmas from which saffron is derived. You will need an awful lot to generate even a tenth of an ounce of saffron.

The bridging crocus is *C. laevigatus* 'Fontenayi' which will flower on and off from November to January. They smell wonderful if you're prepared to lie in the frozen grass to appreciate them. They make a mass of lilac, darker striped on the outside, with a yellow eye and cream anthers; if you mix sources, you should get some flowering in each month.

Move on then to the earliest of the spring-flowering crocus: *C. vernus* 'Vanguard' is appropriately early in a pale silvery blue

and a darker lilac inside.

Recommended for naturalising freely and prolifically are: the standard species of *C. tommasinianus* – a pretty sapphire with delicate veining; *C. t.* 'Ruby Giant' which is actually purple, white flushed from the throat up with big orange stigmas; *C. etruscus* 'Zwanenburg', a light violet; and *C. chrysanthus* 'Cream Beauty' with rounded cream petals and vivid orange stigma creating an egg yolk glow inside the cup. *C. ancyrensis* is also very early and will produce 18 to 24 small brilliant saffron coloured flowers. For the full gamut, plant the giant-flowered varieties to continue later. Zones 4-8. Shown above: *C. tommasinianus*; above left: *C. speciosus*.

CUPRESSUS
Cypress
Cypress is a conifer that needs full sun but will do well on most soils particularly sandy ones. The Kashmir cypress, *C. torulosa* 'Cashmeriana', is a lovely blue weeping willow of a conifer for the bigger garden – it grows to 50ft (15m). Zone 9. The Arizona cypress, *C. arizonica* var. *glabra,* can get almost as high, with a smooth, flaky purple bark and spirals of pungent blue leaves. *C. arizonica* 'Pyramidalis' gets to 35ft (10.5m) and grows fast and pyramidically. Good for a hedge but you'll miss out on the pyramid. Zone 6.

The Monterey cypress, *C. macrocarpa* (*C. m.* 'Silver Dome' is shown above) grows quickly into a column but like us all, it spreads, wider rather than higher. Forms vary between those up to 50ft (15m) and those that grow to 70ft (21m) with a width of oh-my-God 80ft (24m). The best cypress for the smaller garden is the Mediterranean cypress, *C. sempervirens.* Although high – to 50ft (15m) – it is a slim narrow tree, very elegant, and puts you in mind of Dorothy Parker's motto: 'A woman can never be too thin or too rich'. Its grey-bluey green upright foliage and its shape will remind you forever of the Tuscan hills. Zone 9.

CYCLAMEN
Cyclamen
These charming plants of delicacy and modesty, especially compared to their larger greenhouse relations, are members of the primula family. There is a vast range of autumn- and spring-flowering varieties but there are some winter-flowering species too. *C. coum* (shown above) flowers through the winter, purple, cerise, rose-pink, sugar-pink to white, its upright petals and swooping mien suggesting a flock of exotic creatures, somewhere between dragonflies and fairies.

C. coum has rounded dark green leaves, some marbled grey or cream or silver. It prefers a well-drained site, undisturbed for self-seeding, and is extremely hardy, flowering from January to March. Zones 6-9.

You can prolong your winter cyclamen season by also planting *C. persicum*, with or without its splodged pale and dark green leaf – a sort of Rorsach test for gardeners – (to be fair, some varieties have pretty silver marbled leaves) because *persicum* flowers from February to April. It needs a fairly sheltered position. If you're clever you can have cyclamen in every season.

DAPHNE
Daphne
The must-have shrub for the winter garden because of its knock-out scent. *D. mezereum*, known commonly as mezereon, makes a neat 4ft (1.2m) shape and although it is deciduous you would hardly notice, for its branches are covered in clusters of tiny four-petalled tubular stars through late winter and early spring, followed by red fruits. Mezereon is sugar-pink, cerise or purple; *D. m. alba* has creamy white flowers and round yellow fruits. Zones 5-8.

D. odora, the winter daphne is evergreen, sweetly scented, though prone to colds so it needs more shelter. Little bunches of white through to deep pink florets appear from mid winter to early spring. *D. o.* 'Aureomarginata' (shown above) has a band of jersey cream to the leaf edge and deep mauve-pink florets, paler inside (zones 7-9). More exotic, of similar hardiness, is *D. bholua* with longer, leathery leaves and pink to white flowers.

EDGEWORTHIA CHRYSANTHA
Edgeworthia

I have been trying to get hold of this shrub (syn. *E. papyrifera*) ever since I read Sir Peter Smithers' book, Adventures of a Gardener. His story begins like this: '*E. chrysantha* is a small clump-forming shrub sometimes to be found in gardens on the Italian lakes. It is a daphne cousin, and in late winter it carries parchment coloured flowers with a fine fragrance.'

Sir Peter was sent a form of edgworthia, described as 'Mitsumata', by an eminent Japanese plantsman. 'Mitsumata' means 'three branches'. 'As the plant grew the meaning of the name became apparent. At each terminal bud the growth would divide into three... In a couple of years the plant flowered in late January, with flower clusters shading from red in the centre through orange to yellow at the periphery.' His plant is now 8ft (2.4m) high and wide, having survived the heavy frosts of 1985 in Switzerland where he and his edgworthia live: 'Each year it puts on a splendid show. It remains in bloom for a very long time, because the circles of florets open in succession.'

The Japanese yen for it is total: they use it for making currency. Zone 9.

ELAEAGNUS
Oleaster

An evergreen shrub, with a double-whammy leaf: green or variegated on top, silver-white underneath. *E.* x *ebbingei* has a dark green leaf and white back which provides a lovely foil for its fragrant silver-white bells through the later half of autumn. You can get yellow variegated forms if you want them. *E. pungens* 'Maculata' (shown above) is probably the best with a big gold splash in the centre of each leaf, spreading as the leaf grows. Flowers are very fragrant, creamy white. Height and spread about 10ft (3m).

Elaeagnus is often grown free-standing, and *E.* x *ebbingei* makes a good hedge with a height and spread to 15ft (4.5m) but its best use is as a fake climber, trained against a wall. Zones 6-10.

ERANTHIS
Winter aconite

The most hopeful of winter bulbs (tubers, actually), they are small jolly buttercup flowers encircled by dark green jesters' ruffs. They are tough for all their size – a mere 2-4in (5-10cm) high. *E. hyemalis* will start flowering in January, waking wide open in the sunlight and going to sleep in the shade. Zone 4.

Winter aconite does very well on limestone soil and will seed freely, cheering up the bleakest stretch of green, or green-under-snow. It will be as content, though it will probably not naturalise as freely, in a border mixed with other early bulbs, lavender, lilac and blue crocus for example, that open wide and are not too globular.

Like snowdrops (see *Galanthus*) you will have a much greater chance of success if you plant them 'in the green', that is, as clumps of plants which have just finished flowering, not as bulbs. Needless to say they are much more expensive to buy like this. Cultivate friends who grow them in carpets.

ERICA
Heather, heath

Ericas are valuable ground cover: even when they are not in flower their foliage can be spectacular – gold and silver, copper and bronze, ruby and citron. They are excellent for steep banks where attempting to garden regularly would put you in traction for months. They are excellent also for winter containers – bushy, solid colour that no amount of pansies can give. I have an urn which I planted high with rosemary, soft blue-grey-green and clumps of dark rose erica in front. Having said that, I always feel that the natural place for heaths and heathers is moorland and mountain side and a winter garden composed of heathers and dwarf conifers is a poor pastiche of the real thing.

E. carnea 'Pink Spangles'(shown above) has rose-pink and ivory bells from January; *E. c.* 'December Red' is actually a deep pink. These will tolerate lime (zones 5-7). *E. x darleyensis* also lime tolerant: *E. d.* 'Arthur Johnson' grows to 3ft (1m) and bears racemes of mauve flowers from mid winter; *E. d.* 'Silberschmelze', silver-white and fragrant. *E. erigena* is the Irish heath: *E. e.* 'Irish Dusk' has salmon bells and smells of honey. Lime tolerant. Zones 7-8

ERYSIMUM 'BOWLES' MAUVE'
Perennial wallflower

I am not partial to wallflowers but this hardly looks – or smells! – like one. It is an excellent flowerer all year with blue-grey leaves and mauve flowers. It will get woody and leggy as it ages and after only two years or so it will be past its prime. The other side of the coin, however, is that it grows fast, making a 3ft (1m) dome within its first year. You can always take cuttings and, in fact, would be best advised to do so: a very cold winter will kill it off entirely.

The blue delicacy of its flower and leaf colour make it a perfect foil or backdrop for early bulbs: it looks especially good with yellows and deeper violet blues. There are dwarf varieties available also: *E.* 'Moonlight', with yellow flowers, is only 12in (30cm) high but I cannot recommend 'Bowles' Mauve' highly enough. Zone 8.

ERYTHRONIUM
Dog's tooth violet

Darling flower, its petals are wings – rather like cyclamen but even more delicate. I cannot for the life of me see that it resembles dogs' teeth in any way. Strictly speaking this is a spring flower: I include it because you will want to leave room for it.

E. americanum: the typically slender stem, swept back yellow petals with delicate bronze veining and deep bronze anthers. *E. californicum*: pale moonshine yellow and cream anthers with a green and brown tortoise-shell patterned leaf. *E. dens-canis*: pink, white or mauve with a mottled leaf. *E.* 'Pagoda': longer brown stems and a vibrant yellow petal with cinnamon anthers. Zones 4-5.

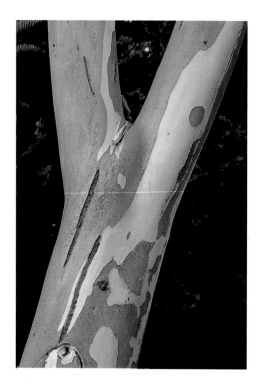

EUCALYPTUS

Gum tree

Not all gums are frost hardy – they need full sun and shelter, especially from cold winds. The young foliage is generally the most attractive and can be perpetuated by cutting growth hard back in the spring.

E. glaucescens (Tingiringi gum) is a lovely, spreading evergreen which is extremely hardy. It grows to 40ft (12m) with a spread of 25ft (7.5m). In youth its bark is pure and white and the young leaves are round and silver-blue, elongating and greying with age. White flowers appear in autumn. Peeling bark (white when young, pink-grey with age) on the mountain gum (*E. dalrympleana*) and brown peeling bark revealing cream on the cider gum (*E. gunnii*). The latter has pretty round silver-blue leaves when young, ageing to a nice blue-green.

The snow gum (*E. pauciflora* ssp. *niphophila*, shown above) is the hardiest with white bark that peels to reveal a snake bark of cinnamon, cream and green. The young shoots are bright red with oval soft grey green leaves which get greyer and narrower with age. Zones 7-9.

EUONYMUS

Euonymus

I can't say I'm mad about this shrub (the common spindle when a tree) and one of these days I'm going to write a book about plants I dislike and why. However, the evergreen varieties are useful in winter. *E. fortunei* 'Emerald Gaiety' grows to 3ft (1m) with a good spread – 5ft (1.5m) and has round leaves edged in cream. It is useful as a hedge or wired against a wall because you can keep cutting it back. If you like green and yellow variegated foliage, you should acquire *E. f.* 'Emerald 'n' Gold'. I don't. It looks brassy and common, like its name.

E. fortunei 'Silver Queen' (shown above) is a different matter. Its glossy green leaf is widely splashed with ivory towards the edge and it bears little bunches of cream bobbles. It will grow to 7ft (2m) or so, and 5ft (1.5m) across. Zones 5-9.

EUPHORBIA

Spurge, milkweed

This is a dependable evergreen perennial for its high, broad slash of colour. *E. characias* ssp. *wulfenii* stands erect, its spikes bearing long blue-green glaucous leaves in the same manner as a bunch of bananas. When the flowers come they look like a mass of lime-green buttons. The flower, in fact, is insignificant: it is the button bract which shields it that catches the eye. They will flower – or button – for four months or so from early spring and stand a good 3ft (1m) high, so it will see through a number of changes in its foreground planting.

E. characias ssp. *characias* is very similar but its flower has a not-so-lovely dark purple centre (zone 8). *E. myrsinites* (shown above) is a sprawler and many people find it unsatisfactory because its flowers will not all bunch together: you will have long strands of thick stem and small fleshy leaves before you get to the exciting bit. But *E. polychroma* is a delight, a dome of about 20in (50cm) and proper flowers of bright yellow surrounded by the green star of its top leaves. Zone 4.

FERNS

Ferns

Strictly speaking, each one should be listed under its own botanical name but I have decided to lump together a choice few and explain the reasons for making them part of the winter garden.

Ferns come in all guises and are suited to different climes. Some are tiny and delicate, some are bold and bossy and bear leaves that are most unfern-like, for example, *Asplenium nidus* (the bird's nest fern) in a strange yellowy green colour, up to 4ft (1.2m) high, and not the slightest hint of a cut or feathery leaf. The best really big fern grows like a palm tree: *Dicksonia antarctica*, the Australian tree fern (shown above). Most books stipulate that this plant is half hardy, tolerating temperatures down to only 0°C or 32°F but I have seen them established in many places where the temperature drops well below this point. They are very, very beautiful.

Ferns are very useful for damp shady places, green and tranquil to look at when the skies are grey, magic when the frost comes. The following are all fully evergreen and fully hardy: *Blechnum capense* has arching spreading fronds, grows 18in

(45cm) high and is good for mixing with other foliage. *Polystichum munitum* (the giant holly fern) grows 4ft (1.2m) high with shiny dark green fronds. *Polypodium vulgare* 'Cornubiense' has a delicate, well cut leaf of fresh green and a height and spread of only 12in (30cm), if that, and looks pretty when mixed with woodland bulbs, like the white *Anemone nemorosa*. *Polypodium cambricam* is shown above.

FESTUCA GLAUCA

Blue fescue

This is an evergreen and, in fact, silver-blue grass that makes lovely, even tufts of about 10in (25cm). It should be divided every two or three years in the spring. It needs full sun to keep its blue rinse going, otherwise it will revert to green, and it needs a well-drained soil or it will die from sogginess. Drought is its joy. These plants are good as stoppers at the front of a border. Shear over in winter to remove dying foliage.
Zones 4-8.

FORSYTHIA
Forsythia
A rush of yellow flowers – from lemon to deep honey-gold – on bare stems in very early spring and then it's all over. Forsythias have inconsequential foliage for the most part although *F.* x *intermedia* 'Karl Sax' has the advantage of red to purple leaf in the autumn and is also a good, prolific flowerer. It grows densely to about 8ft (2.4m). *F. suspensa* and its varieties will root wherever the tips touch the ground.

However, forsythias need not sprawl all over the place, taking up room just because of their annual show. You can train them against a wall, or more unusually grow them as standards, so that in flower you will have a golden globe on a slim stem. Trim well. Zones 5-9.

GALANTHUS
Snowdrop
The purest, most delicate of early winter flowers, hiding their faces with a modest downwards glance, the outer petals often shielding a green-frilled or double inner cup. There are hundreds of species, did you know? As any Snowdrop Queen will tell you, you can time them for a perfect run straight through from autumn to early summer.

That's outside the scope of this book, but here are a few varieties to play with. *G. nivalis* (the common snowdrop) has narrow green strap leaves and a pendant flower hanging from its green holder by a thread; *G. nivalis* 'Sandersii' has a yellow holder, and yellow flush to the apex of its inner petals, but so enclosed is it by its long outer petals, it resembles most closely the pure white drop. *G. n.* 'Flore Pleno' is altogether jollier, the double common snowdrop, with white and often green frilled many petalled underskirts. *G. elwesii* has blue-green wider leaves and green inner petals. *G. nivalis* 'Viridapicis' has a little green arrow on its inner petals and a flush of green at the tip of its outer petals. *G.* 'S Arnott' is shown above. All these begin in January. Zone 4.

GARRYA ELLIPTICA
Silk tassel bush
A native Californian evergreen shrub with dark olive leaves, desirable principally for its winter adornment of long drooping clusters of soft grey-green catkins. But it is the male rather than the female variety which wears the jewellery. Go for the variety *G. e.* 'James Roof' (shown above) whose catkins on established plants will grow from late autumn onwards reaching 12-16in (30-40cm) in mid winter to early spring.

Whilst the silk tassel bush looks lovely when in tassel, it is the most incredibly boring shrub in summer when all you have to look at is a mass of dreary dark leaves. In this state it is also extremely depressing. Jolly it up by planting a summer-flowering climber to run through it: *Clematis* 'Gravetye Beauty' is vigorous and prolific with lots of small bright red flowers like open tulips through summer and early autumn.

Although it looks tough, it needs shelter and the young plants burn easily in cold winds. It hates to be moved so choose its home carefully - in any well-drained soil, preferably by a wall, in full sun. It has good resistance to atmospheric pollution and salty sea breezes. Zone 8.

GAULTHERIA
Partridge or checker berry
An evergreen shrub, originating in America, useful for landscaping in virtue of its ability to cover large tracts of ground via underground stems. It positively hates lime so you must have an acid soil. *G. procumbens* is the sub-shrub to go for if you want groundcover, its shiny, leathery leaves turning bronze, purple and green in winter. In summer it carries pale pink flowers in the leaf axils, followed by red berries in autumn often lasting through the winter.

For more compact versions try *G. cuneata* with nodding white hearts in summer and white berries in autumn or *G. miqueliana* with pale pink bell flowers, up to six to a stem, in late spring and pink or white fruits. *G. shallon* drops racemes of pink and white hearts in summer and deep purple berries in autumn. Zones 3-8.

HAKONECHLOA
Hakonechloa
One of those splendid grasses that make handsome tufts. *H. macra* 'Aureola' has purple stems and long green and yellow striped leaves that turn red and gold with age. Open panicles of feathery red and gold flower spikes appear in autumn, lasting through the winter. Height 16in (40cm), spread to 24in (60cm).

H. m. 'Alboaurea' (shown above) starts off with similar green and yellow stripes but turns into a feathery, straw-coloured dome. Slow-growing, it is a good plant for winter containers. Zones 7-9.

HAMAMELIS
Witch hazel
A large and lovely family of deciduous trees and shrubs which offers virtues in every season. Brilliant glowing foliage in autumn and leafless branches to be decorated with raggle-taggle gypsy flowers of pale yellow, gold, orange, copper to crimson between mid winter and early spring. Almost all are deliciously fragrant and the flowers are never harmed by frost.

H. x *intermedia* is a hybrid group of which 'Feuerzauber' has the most brilliant crimson autumn leaves while those of 'Diane' are yellow and red. 'Orange Beauty' (shown above), has rich orange flowers. Height and spread 8-10ft (2.4-3m). Zones 5-9.

H. mollis is the Chinese witch hazel, an open shrub with a downy green leaf, glowing yellow in autumn. Deep yellow flowers and bronze sepals persist through winter. Height and spread to 12ft (3.6m). Zones 5-9.

H. vernalis 'Sandra' bears deep yellow spider blooms in late winter, followed by young purple leaves turning mid green in summer and a rainbow in autumn – purple, red, orange and yellow (zones 4-9). They all dislike chalk and need a good mulch, leafmould or humus, every other year.

HEBE
Veronica

A remarkable range of evergreen shrubs with assorted flowering times, shapes and sizes. Smaller, more compact domes are excellent for containers, like *H. pinguifolia* with its blue-grey leaves. *H.* 'Autumn Glory' makes a low dome 2ft (60cm) high to just over 2½ft (75cm) wide. Red shoots bear rounded blue-green leaves and racemes of violet flowers from mid summer to early winter.

H. x *franciscana* 'Blue Gem' is spreading, 2ft (60cm) high and 4ft (1.2m) wide with a dense arrangement of oblong leaves and equally dense spikes of violet flowers from mid summer to early winter. *H.* 'Red Edge' (shown above) has eponymous tips to its glaucous leaves in winter and spring. It makes a little mound, height and spread to about 18in (45cm). Hardiness varies; it is not reliable in cold northern temperate climes. Roughly zones 8-11, but check with your supplier.

HEDERA
Ivy

Ivies are among the most useful of winter woollies, wrapping walls and fences and bare ground in shades of green, or splashed with gold, silver, copper or cream. Their variegation is like a fingerprint. You will find that no one pattern is identical with another.

Unusual winter ivies include *H. helix* 'Atropurpurea' whose dark green triangular leaves turn a glossy maroon-purple in winter, highlighted by its paler green veining. A similar transformation happens to *H. h.* 'Glymii' which has more heart-shaped leaves. *H. h.* 'Buttercup' has light green leaves that turn butter yellow in full sun. *H. h.* 'Glacier' has a delightful small tri-lobed leaf in a soft bluey green with a silver patina and flashes of ivory and is notably frost-resistant. *H. hibernica* 'Gracilis' turns a brilliant copper red in autumn that warms a wall all winter through. It is not suitable as groundcover but will attain a height of 15ft (4.5m) or more.

The most surprising ivy is *H. helix* 'Conglomerata'. It grows free standing, making a bush of 3ft (1m) with erect stems and curly leaves. All zones 4-9.

HELLEBORUS
Christmas rose, Lenten rose

In recent years, these plants have become terribly fashionable and much more widely obtainable. A wonderfully useful perennial for its winter flowers whose subtle, reticent colours belie its dreadfully promiscuous nature.

Begin with a bed of *H. foetidus* (shown above, zones 6-9) with its pale green, creamy cups hanging modestly down; add a few *H. niger* or Christmas rose (zones 4-8), nodding white cups with a heart of gold stamens, *H. orientalis* (zones 4-9) with dusty pink petals spotted a darker hue on the inside, and in a few years there will be great confusion as to which progeny resulted from what parents.

Good in most soils, better in a north-facing, shaded position, they benefit from a light humus mulch if the soil is dry. They don't mind wet ground.

HEPATICA

Liverwort

Named for its traditional medicinal uses as a liver cure, though it would be unwise to go nibbling at it with the next hangover, this is a family of evergreen or semi-evergreen herbaceous perennials whose flowers appear in late winter to early spring before the new leaves are fully formed.

H. x *media* 'Ballardii' grows – slowly – into a dome of intense blue flowers about 4in (10cm) high with a spread of 12in (30cm) of pretty wavy-edged leaves. It likes semi shade because its origins are the woodlands of the north temperate zone.

H. nobilis (syn. *Anemone hepatica* and *Triloba*) var. *japonica* betrays its close relationship to the anemone even more clearly with shallow cups of brilliant lavender-blue flowers (though you can get it also in pink or white), a green eye and lots of delicate mauve stamens. Zone 7.

HEUCHERA

Alum root

This herbaceous perennial in the form known as *H. micrantha* var. *diversifolia* 'Palace Purple' (shown above) was introduced from America and is good value for the winter garden. It makes clumps of bronze plum leaves of a glossy paper texture which persist through winter. In summer it bears sprays of tiny white flowers on high thin stems, rather like London pride.

Many will say it makes good groundcover but to use it as such would both do the plant a disservice and be a waste of its potential. Covering vast areas of ground with a lot of brown leaves will make it look like autumn. Use the plant sparingly and set with a contrasting colour to highlight its rich tones. I have planted one of my winter tubs this year with three heuchera plants surrounding a clump of heather, *Calluna vulgaris* 'Silver Knight' whose woolly silver wands will purple as winter progresses, and interspersed white winter pansies to lift and highlight the richer colours. Zones 4-8.

HYACINTHUS

Hyacinth

Every winter and seemingly all winter my maternal grandmother's house was filled with the scent of hyacinths. Mostly they were blue – she had a passion for blue – and in summer there were vases of pale mauve scabious everywhere. Now I, too, need to fill my house with their high, dry scent, an invigorating antidote to the urge to hibernate.

You can buy 'treated' bulbs for forcing indoors. Plant in a cool dark place, not over 45°F for six to eight weeks and do not bring them in until the flower spike is 2-3in (5-8cm) high. This ensures a strong root system and sturdy flowering. Outdoor ones are spring flowerers: they benefit particularly from staking – alongside the stem and pierced straight into the bulb.

Whilst hyacinths' individual florets are charming, the cylindrical shape of the entire flower spike is not. The solution is to bung them in all together in all one colour and all of the same variety. Placed by a door or window they will bring their scent inside. Or try the multiflora varieties whose bells are set on several slender stems. 'Blue Princess' and 'Snow Princess' are the prettiest.

ILEX
Holly

Conventionally a 'typical' winter tree or shrub, but I am not a huge fan, largely because of their prickles. However, there are a number seriously spinally-challenged and all the better for it. Most hollies are either male or female. If you want a female to berry you will have to plant a male nearby.

I. x altaclerensis 'Camelliifolia' has lots of advantages: vigorous, evergreen, frost hardy, resistant to coastal exposure and pollution; it has long, elegant glossy leaves, most of which are spine free. The young stems are a nice purple and it can be relied upon to produce lots of fat, round, red berries. Its habit is narrow and pyramidal with a height to 46ft (14m) and spread of 10ft (3m). Female.

I. cornuta (horned holly, shown above) is an evergreen rounded shrub to a height of 12ft (3.6m). *I. c.* 'Burfordii' has only one horn at the tip of its very shiny leaf, produces masses of fruits and spreads to 8ft (2.4m); female. *I. crenata* (box-leaved holly) is a good hedger with small oval leaves, rounded teeth and shiny black fruits. Height to 15ft (4.5m), spread 10ft (3m). *I. glabra* (inkberry) has similar berries and smooth leaves. Height to 8ft (2.4m), spread 6ft (1.8m). Zones 5-9.

IRIS
Iris

The tiny bulb irises are perfect for February flowers. *I. danfordiae* is a mountain iris with a gaping yellow mouth like a baby cuckoo – actually it's very attractive and looks wonderful with the deep blue *I. reticulata* (shown above) from whose group it springs. It is into fertility in a big way, producing lots of tiny bulblets so its needs to be planted deep, up to 8in (20cm). Zones 4-9.

I. foetidissima travels under a variety of names, none of them very appealing: gladwin or gladdon iris, roastbeef plant, and from the Latin, stinking iris. Its charm lies not in its summer flowers, a plain yellow or dull purple, but in its striking scarlet seed pods and bright orange fruits which you will find hanging between its long, strappy green leaves. Zones 5-9.

I. histrioides has complex patterning, its fall spotted in dark blue and white with a yellow blaze. *I. h.* 'Major' is a dark blue violet, 'Lady Beatrix Stanley' pale blue (zones 4-9). The sweetly scented *Iris reticulata* flowers in February, only 6in (15cm) high with a royal purple flower with a golden blaze. These, with *I. danfordiae*, are my favourites. Zones 4-9.

JASMINUM NUDIFLORUM
Winter-flowering jasmine

This is a jolly good shrub if supported against a wall, otherwise it can tend to get very sprawly and out of hand. The small, bright yellow starry masses like tiny petalled trumpets will smother the green leafless stems if you prune it well after flowering. It layers naturally.

Jasmine needs full sun and reasonably well-drained soil. No doubt it does better in fertile soil but over the years and various gardens, I've neglected quite a few in my time and they have nevertheless rewarded me by fantastic winter displays. It has a height and spread of up to 10ft (3m) so take care where you place it. Zones 6-9.

JUNIPERUS

Juniper

These are an extremely varied lot. I
personally will have nothing to do with
those that repose in the immortal words of
Lady Bracknell, in a 'semi-recumbent
posture' probably because a conifer's
foliage does not look well sprawling over
the ground. *J. horizontalis* is the creeping
juniper, a depressing green, and *J. communis*
'Aureopicta' is an equally depressing
yellow, darker in winter, semi prostrate.

Far more like it is the Irish juniper, *J.
communis* 'Hibernica' (shown above). It is a
nice narrow, upright tapering column,
growing to between 10 and 15ft (3-4.5m)
but only about 12in (30cm) in diameter. Its
needles are dense and aromatic and its
berries take three years to mature from
green through blue to black. You can clip
them to accentuate their conicality or keep
them smaller; they will grow in any soil and
they are jolly tough, the perfect stand-in for
the Italian cypress in colder climes.
Zones 5-8.

LARIX KAEMPFERI

Japanese larch

L. k. 'Diane' is another of those contorted
branch trees like Harry Lauder's Walking
Stick (see *Corylus avellana* 'Contorta') but
only half the height and spread (to about 4ft
or 1.2 m). It has curly leaves in a pale green
which go gold in autumn, dropping off in
winter to reveal its branches.

Clothed with a heavy frost it looks as if it
has had a nice perm and a silver rinse.
Perhaps because its shape is much less
agonised than the corylus, perhaps because
it is so much smaller, I find this quite a
pretty tree. It makes a good centrepiece in
the corner of a small garden. Zones 5-7.

LAURUS

Bay tree, bay laurel

Laurus nobilis is the sweet bay, or bay laurel
which is entirely delightful and not to be
confused with the gloomy laurels beloved
of the Victorians (*Prunus lusitanica* and
Aucuba japonica). It is an extremely obliging
evergreen shrub or tree which will give you
a year round supply of aromatic leaves for
cooking and will happily be clipped into
pyramids, balls or lollipop standards. Its
leaf is a handsome dark glossy green.

You are much more likely these days to
see the bay grown in containers. This is
because they are not totally frost hardy.
Their leaves can be burnt or you can lose
the plant entirely, as I once did, overnight,
in extreme cold. They will need some form
of shelter or protection if the temperature is
going to drop hard.

The big bay trees you see, often at a gate,
going on some 40ft (12m) will be inured
over many years to the worst of winters.
They will be old – it is a slow-growing tree
– and take everything in their stride.
Zones 8-11.

LEUCOJUM
Snowflake
L. vernum (shown above) is the spring snowflake, like a biggish snowdrop, hanging one or two pretty white bells with green tips. It grows about 6in (15cm) high but will double that if the weather is warm. Needless to say, it likes a sunny spot.

L. vernum flowers in February. It naturalises well in grass – a great drift of them is a lovely thing to see – but it looks pretty also in clumps with other late winter bulbs. The trick is to get them overhanging the other flowers. Any that are delicate in form that will lift their faces up to the snowflake's bell will look well with it. Delicate crocus, like *C. vernus* ssp. *albiflorus* with white faces and yellow stamens, or *C. sieberi* 'Albus', which has a waterlily shape and a golden throat and stamens are delightful in clumps on their own anyway. The thing is to get them flowering at the same time. Zone 5.

LONICERA
Honeysuckle
The genus has some wildly disparate forms. You would hardly think that a small-leaved bushy evergreen shrub was in any way related to the climber that produces the long curving tubules of flowers with which William Morris patterned the chintzes of middle England in the late nineteenth century.

L. fragrantissima is one of the loveliest winter flowerers. Delicate cream and white flowers with long stamens burst into flower all along reddish stems from about December onwards. It is a wonderfully penetrating scent so a few stems in a glass indoors will easily banish winter oppression.

Equally splendid scent comes from the cream flowers of *L. x purpusii* 'Winter Beauty' (shown above right; *L. x purpusii* above) raised by Hillier's foreman Alf Alford by backcrossing *L. x purpusii* with *L. standishii*. They say the good die young: this variety doesn't die but it flowers best when young - often from December to early April. Well worth replacing in middle age. *L. standishii* has bristly stems, and pink flushed flowers in winter.

These honeysuckles are unremarkable bushy things the rest of the year, spreading to 12ft (3.6m) with half that height but it will play host to other climbers through it, like clematis, for flowering later in the year. Zones 5-9.

L. nitida, by contrast, is not something nasty which gets into children's hair, but is a dense bushy evergreen which can be a useful substitute for box because it grows faster and is amenable to clipping. If you don't clip it, its branches will arch all over the place in a fairly shaggy manner but tiny cream flowers, also fragrant, will appear all over it in late spring. *L. n.* 'Baggesen's Gold' is the yellow version. Zones 7-9.

LUNARIA ANNUA
Honesty

This a summer-flowering biennial which you must find a place for in your winter garden. When in autumn you pick off the outer cases of its seedpods – it is a three-layer arrangement with the seeds as filling for a triple-decker sandwich – you will find the middle layer which is its 'penny'. Silver-white, translucent and burnished like the most fragile mother-of-pearl, the pennies will persist through wind and rain and snow.

I used to grow honesty only for its winter decorations, putting up with its vulgar purple flowers and undistinguished leaf until I saw the most beautiful variety growing in a friend's garden. All white flowers, and plenty of them, with a well-cut leaf whose fine tips might have had icing sugar sifted over them. With typical generosity he gave me not one but several plants. I went home, ripped out all the others, for fear of cross-breeding, and planted them where they would light a semi-shaded corner both with spring flowers and winter mother-of-pearl. And I forgot they were biennial. So the following year I had none. A cautionary tale for those who want annual flowering. Zone 4.

MAGNOLIA
Magnolia

One of the most beautiful, if not the most beautiful, trees in the world for its waxy goblets or waterlilies in ivory, cream, rose and deep violet. Its sculptured petals, its subtle tones of colour make it perfect. Or almost. There is one species which is commonly but erroneously assumed to be the only winter-flowering species which I do not rate and that is the white form of *M. stellata* (syn. *M. tomentosa*). Its white is harsh, cold and clinical and whilst it might look pretty against blue summer skies surrounded by fresh green foliage, it looks depressingly sterile in late February or March.

Perhaps the best is *M. campbellii* (the Himalayan 'pink tulip tree') whose enormous goblets, deep rose pink outside, paler within, open into wide waterlilies in February through March. But you will have to be either very philanthropic or very patient: this tree needs a good 15-20 years before it flowers – or more! *M. c.* ssp. *mollicomata* is an excellent substitute, needing only about 10 years. Zone 9.

MAHONIA
Mahonia

Mahonias are evergreen shrubs which range from the spectacular to the indescribably boring like *M. aquifolium* (the Oregon grape) whose leaves turn purple in winter and has bunches of small yellow flowers in spring. Mine has mildew instead.

Of the spectacular varieties, I once had a *M. japonica* which I inherited with the garden. It had a handsome form, deep shiny green leaves – and prickles which I overlooked. From autumn to spring it bore masses of scented pale yellow flowers in racemes and lovely blue berries in summer. I loved it but it was in the wrong place. Evidently the person who had planted it had not thought it would grow to a width approaching 10ft (3m) and a height of 5ft (1.5m). I thought it was too old to move – and it was. Zones 7-9.

M. x media 'Charity' is more widely sold. The flowers are a much harder yellow held up as a hand rather than hanging in sprays. *M. x media* 'Roundwood' (shown above) is a rich, golden colour. Zones 8-9.

MALUS
Crab apple

The crab apple is a delight for the eyes as well as the stomach. Profusely blossoming in spring, it has wonderful red, yellow or apricot fruits in autumn, some varieties hanging on well into winter even when all the leaves have long given up the ghost. And as to the stomach, they make the most delicious jelly.

Good varieties for persisting into winter are: 'Golden Hornet', 'Red Jade', 'Red Sentinel' and *M.* x *robusta*. The first will give you, briefly, branches wreathed in pure white blossom in spring which, come the autumn, will have turned into tiny golden apples and look rather as if bunches of gold grapes have been tied along their length.

'Red Jade' comes from Brooklyn Botanic Garden originally. In late spring it will give you tight pink buds concealing white flowers, to be exchanged later for an abundance of shiny little cherries which last well. 'Red Sentinel' has soldiers' scarlet jacketed fruits which last until spring. *Robusta* has scarlet fruits and like 'Golden Hornet' it will take the severest frost to dislodge them. Birds willing, their fruits will be there till February. All zone 5.

MISCANTHUS
Silver grass

A whole range of grasses, from 2ft (60cm) to 10ft (3m), mostly clump forming. Although it is known as silver grass, remember that not all that glitters is silver. *M. sinensis* 'Zebrinus' (shown above), for example, suffers from broad gold stripes which are horizontal, detracting from the arcing vertical elegance of the plant.

M. s. 'Variegatus', however, has vertical white stripes which allow the plant a handsome decoration appropriate to its stature – 5ft (1.5m) high and 3ft (1m) broad. *M. s.* 'Gracillimus' makes a clump of the finest narrow arching leaves of a brilliant emerald green. It may or may not flower in autumn, though it may go quite bronze, and grows to about 4ft (1.2m) by 18in (45cm). Miscanthus is not evergreen but its green lasts well until the winter really bites when the tufts of gold or straw or bronze will look magic under frost. Zones 7-9.

MUSCARI
Grape hyacinth

The good old-fashioned spikes of tight blue bells have undergone a small revolution in recent years and are now to be found in sickly shades of pink as well as white, yellow, shades of mauve and even green. If you can be bothered to get down in the mud on your hands and knees you will find it smells very sweetly. The obvious way to enjoy its scent is to plant it in bowls for the house.

A most obliging bulb, muscari will thrive anywhere in any kind of soil, in sun or partial shade. Use it thickly either side of the length of a path, mix it in clumps between heather, or again clumped between groups of miniature golden narcissus.

Most muscari are spring flowering. Earlier forms are *M. azureum* (shown above) with tight heads of powder blue which flower in March or *M. armeniacum* 'Blue Pearl' which can be forced into cobalt blue bloom in January if planted early. Zone 4.

NARCISSUS
Narcissus

Out of this huge family, lovely and varied, (and what would we do without our daffs?) you will find that there are not that many which will qualify for inclusion in a winter garden, but amongst the earliest are:

N. asturiensis – miniature with waisted pendent sunshine trumpets; N. 'Brunswick' – elegant proportions, white perianth with a pale buttermilk crown; N. bulbocodium (hoop petticoat) – a conical cup encircled by spikes rather than petals, not obviously a narcissus, pale lemon or gold; N. cyclamineus – reflexed 'petals' of the perianth stand straight up above the long hanging trumpet and look for all the world like a collection of miniature chefs' tocques in yellow. An acquired taste. N. 'February Silver' – milk petals and warm lemon trumpets; N. 'Peeping Tom' – early but extraordinary: swooped back petals and horizontal trumpets which are very long and nosy. They look like a bunch of jaundiced paparazzi when you see them en masse; N. 'Tête-à-Tête' – two or three butter yellow trumpets, shown above; N. triandrus – milk-white with swooping reflexed petals and a tear drop trumpet.

OPHIOPOGON
Ophiopogon

Ophiopogon planiscapus 'Nigrescens' is an evergreen perennial but looks like black grass. A splendidly alternative plant, it makes clumps about 12in (30cm) wide and 9in (23cm) high and will spread. A very useful foil for other plants and looks dramatic when set with blue, pink, pale yellow or white early bulbs.

It is also good with a host of other plants: Ajuga reptans 'Multicolor' because of its very purplish leaf blotched with cream and pink; and with Helleborus orientalis with its dusty pink-purple cups hanging over the black blades.

Ophiopogon has racemes of lilac flowers in summer then black fruits. Zone 8.

OSMANTHUS
Osmanthus

Literally fragrant flower, this family of evergreen shrubs and trees is remarkable for its scent and if I had a big enough garden I would make a national collection of all its different species. My reward would be their heady scent for much of the year.

Osmanthus is a native of the southern United States and Asia and some species require shelter. The species for winter flowers, or rather late winter flowers, is half tree, half shrub. O. yunnanensis (syn. O. forrestii) begins as a tree with an upright stem and then spreads as a shrub. Its long lance leaves in a dark olive-green may be both wavy and toothed as well as smooth and flat. The flowers are ivory. Their fragrance is almost addictive. Height and spread, though very slowly, to 30ft (9m), it roughly makes 12ft (3.6m) of growth in the first ten years. Hardy in a sheltered spot.

Other species make a valuable addition for their attractive evergreen foliage. O. heterophyllus is rather like a holly with glossy, spiny leaves. O. h. 'Purpureus' has purple-tinged foliage, while that of 'Variegatus' (shown above) is edged with cream. Zones 8-10.

PARROTIA PERSICA

Persian ironwood

This is a member of the witch hazel family (see *Hamamelis*) so you will not be surprised by its strange vivid red flowers in late winter, beginning as a tight cluster of small deep orange fingers, actually stamens, breaking from round brown bracts.

Its branches reach up and arc over, some down to the ground, and its foliage, a rich green in summer, turns a wonderful rainbow of yellow, orange, crimson and purple in autumn. The bark is nice: flaky, fawn and taupe. Oxford University's Botanic Gardens have a magnificent specimen, glorious in flower. Height and spread to 30ft (9m). Zones 6-9.

PERNETTYA

Pernettya

A family of evergreen shrubs, often listed as *Gaultheria*, originating in the area between Mexico and the south of South America. They cannot tolerate a lime soil. Their flowers are tiny but prolific and result in clusters of extraordinary berries that look exactly like the plastic bobbles you find on children's hair ornaments, in a range of colours from white through to purple.

P. mucronata is the showiest. It makes excellent groundcover with its spreading mass of wiry stems to between 2 and 3ft (60-90cm) high and nearly 5ft (1.5m) in spread. A host of little white bells in May and June leave the plant densely packed with bobbles. *P. m.* 'Atrococcinea' is well-named for its large shining cochineal red berries; 'Lilian' has large mauve-pink berries; 'Mulberry Wine' magenta ripening to deep purple; 'Sea Shell' shell-pink to rose and 'Wintertime' large pure white berries (shown above). A delightfully vulgar shrub. Zones 7-9.

PETASITES

Petasites

A space age or jungly perennial with vast leaves looking wonderful by water. The entrancing thing about this plant is that it is such a con. It begins, oh so innocently, with a small posy of tightly packed rosettes in late winter or early spring depending on the species. This is why they are here: they look attractive but slightly unnerving – their geometry is just that bit too perfect. They open as daisies. Then the foliage appears and before you know it, gigantic pale green soup plates are held aloft on 5ft (1.5m) high stems, each leaf as wide as the stem is long.

P. fragrans (shown above) is the winter heliotrope, only 12in (30cm) high but it has a spread respectable among petasites, of 4ft (1.2m). It flowers in late winter with pinky white daisy heads with a scent of vanilla pods which is rather alluring. Leaves are dark green.

P. japonicus var. *giganteus*, the giant butterbur, is the more astonishing. Its flowers emerge in early spring. Their rootspread helps to bind clay banks of ponds and streams but it is invasive. You have been warned! Zone 5.

PHORMIUM
New Zealand flax

An evergreen perennial that looks exotic but is hardy (some more than others), does well despite coastal exposure or urban pollution and grows as a handsome clump of swords. Be careful placing this plant as it does look exotic even though it has naturalised all over the west of Ireland.

P. tenax is the most architectural, growing to 10ft (3m) with a spread up to 6ft (1.8m). Its shape is similar to the yucca but its summer flowers (red) are nowhere near as striking, although it produces a lot of them between its stiff dark green leaves.

There are many varieties crossed with *P. cookianum* (the smaller, laxer of the two species) in green and yellow, green and cream, red, pink and yellow in varying degrees of garishness. They also tend to be less hardy. Restrained types include *P. t.* 'Purpureum' with dark purplish copper leaves, a spread of 3ft (1m) and a height between 6 and 8ft (1.8-2.4m). *P.* 'Bronze Baby' is much smaller and prettier with a height and spread to 2ft (60cm), but its leaves are a bluey wine colour. Zones 9-10.

PICEA
Spruce

The spruce is among the most ornamental of evergreen conifers, owing partly to its shape: usually conical; its colours: green, blue, gold and silver; its branches: whorls; and its cones: ripening in their first autumn but hanging on till their second which means there are almost always some about.

P. abies is the Norway spruce. It is also the Christmas tree so if you are making an archetypal winter garden you had better have one. They don't all grow to the size of the tree that Norway sends to England every year, though it is very kind of them and looks wonderful in Trafalgar Square.

P. a. procera 'Glauca' is conical, holding its branches of blue foliage in tiers from a silver trunk. Eventual height 50ft (15m). *P. a.* 'Finedonensis' is a small pretty tree, with spreading, silver branches. *P. a.* 'Pyramidata' is good for the small garden, high and narrow with upswept branches. Zones 3-7.

P. pungens is the magnificent Colorado spruce. Cultivars include the exceptional *P. p.* 'Globosa' (shown above), a spreading tree, but it can be pruned to a neat pyramid. Silver winter needles are renewed in spring to a fresh blue. To 2ft (60cm).

PIERIS JAPONICA
Pieris

If you have an acid soil, this is a winter garden must. Pieris is hung in winter with ropes of pearls – panicles of white, ivory or blush bells – by the handful. Most flower from February or March and on during April, but the inflorescence, the raceme, often developing in the autumn, is frequently purplish red or pink and attractive before the flowers even open.

It is a nice dense, rounded bushy shrub, a high dome in outline usually growing to between 6 and 10ft (1.8-3m). The glossy green foliage is coppery when young. *P. j.* 'Blush' is one of the first pink varieties with dark shiny green leaves, rose buds opening white, flushed delicately with pink. 'Daisen' is a selection from Mount Daisen in Japan. The buds are deep pink opening paler. 'Red Mill' is North American and extremely hardy. The young leaves are bronze red turning to dark green and the flowers are white. 'Coleman' is shown above.

P. j. 'Christmas Cheer' is very hardy and very early and the shell-pink flowers are flushed carmine at their tips. Even young plants are clever enough to produce their flowers in abundance. Zones 6-8.

PINUS
Pine

Lovely but, like spruce, impossible to cover them all. I'd have Scots pines and Corsican pines if I could, but then I'd also have Douglas fir and the odd giant redwood or two.

Having said that, the Scots pine is jolly slow growing and is tolerant of all soils and sites, so a young one needn't be out of the question. A good and unusual sort of pine for a medium garden is the lace-bark pine, *Pinus bungeana* (shown above). It grows slowly making several upright branches from the main trunk; the overall effect is triangular. The irregular intervals between the foliage reveal glimpses of its lovely bark, an exquisite grey which flakes to reveal a dappled green and cream underside, darkening to a bluish red. The needles are aromatic. Height to around 30ft (9m), but slowly, and spread to a little over half that. Zones 5-8.

POPULUS TREMULA
Aspen

The rustling flutter of aspen leaves when the wind whispers through them is reason enough to plant one in your garden. But it has other advantages: the colour cycle of its foliage – bronze-red when young, grey-green when adult and butter yellow in autumn; and its catkins – long and grey, they drape the branchlets in late winter to early spring. It can get to 50ft (15m) with a spread of 30ft (9m).

P. t. 'Erecta' is upright, with a spread of 15ft (4.5m). *P. t.* 'Pendula' is the weeping form, much smaller – height between 15 and 30ft (4.5-9m) – and with an abundance of mulberry-coloured male catkins in February. *P. tremuloides*, the American aspen, is of roughly the same height as the weeping aspen, the young bark being an attractive pale yellow and both its leaves and catkins are more slender and finer. At home it extends from the mountains of northern Mexico northwards to Alaska. Fully hardy.

PRIMULA VULGARIS
Primrose

The sweetest flower of all, with its pale hopeful face, modest mien and humble leaf, it shows tremendous courage, pushing through early in the year. Everything about this little plant shows honour and optimism. Primrose takes her name from the Latin appellation of the Middle Ages – Prima rosa – the first rose.

As a child I had been used to seeing our primroses in the dell, which was semi wild, and I find it difficult now to see it treated as a cultivated, over-gardened member of the beds and borders. It is inherently a wild flower and a free spirit. But they do make pretty clumps, it must be said. Allow them a little of their own nature and grow them under a tree or on a grassy bank.

Cultivars include *P. v.* 'Alba Plena' with double white flowers; *P. v.* ssp. *sibthorpii* which is pale pink with a lemon eye. Zone 6.

Other species of primula appear later, such as *P. denticulata*. With its mauve pompoms on long stalks it is much more at home in borders, but hardly to be considered in the same breath.

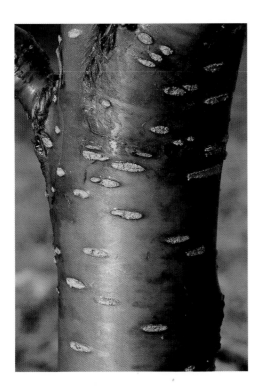

PRUNUS

Cherry tree

Cherry blossom in winter is guaranteed to lift the spirits and when the wind sends wave upon wave of white petals blowing across the window you might be forgiven for thinking a heavenly snow storm had arisen.

Outstandingly good early flowering cherries derive from *P. incisa*, the Fuji cherry, with clusters of white blossom, often delicately pink veined and a flush of pink stamens. It makes a good shrub or a small tree and can even be used for hedging. *P. i.* 'February Pink' is a small spreading tree, height and width to about 25ft (7.5m) giving you lots of little pink flowers in February or even earlier. *P. i.* 'Praecox' is about the same size and bears pale pink buds which open white. Zone 6.

P. mume is the Japanese apricot bearing single pink flowers which smell of almonds. It is extremely pretty and may flower as early as January – or not, for it is not one of those plants that necessarily do things by the book. It is however quite versatile, happy to be a specimen tree or to be trained against a warm wall. *P. m.* 'Alboplena' has semi-double white flowers in late winter or early spring. *P. m.* 'Beni-chidori' is a beautiful rich crimson (shown above). Zones 7-9.

P. subhirtella 'Autumnalis' is the autumn cherry which needs renaming at once: it flowers intermittently with lovely semi-double white blossom, pink in bud, on leafless stems during mild spells from November to March. *P. s.* 'Autumnalis Rosea' is the pink form. It will make a large shrub or small tree to 20ft (6m). Zones 5-8.

The other prunus to go for in winter is *P. serrula* originating in Western China. It has willow leaves and small white flowers in April, but its bark is glorious all year with all the depth and patina of polished mahogany. I have known owners so devoted to this slim, elegant piece of wood, a sort of living torchère, that they insist on improving upon nature with a can of furniture polish and a duster. *P. maackii* 'Amber Beauty' is shown above left. Zone 6.

PULMONARIA

Lungwort

If someone tells you they have got pulmonaria do not offer them penicillin but ask if you can have a bit. It is a clump-forming perennial that is famed for its spotty leaves and pink and blue flowers on the same plant. But not all versions have spots and not all are pink and blue.

P. 'Mawson's Blue' has narrow mid green leaves after the early delicate deep blue flower that looks like a miniature borage (and tinges red with age, I admit). Height and spread about 9in (23cm). Zones 3-8.

P. rubra opens even earlier – in January – with a rosy pink flower and, again, spotless leaves. It makes a bigger clump: height to 12in (30cm) and spread 24in (60cm). Zones 5-8.

P. saccharata (shown above), the Bethlehem sage, has the spotted leaves; *P. s.* 'Alba' flowers very early in whatever weather and has white flowers. *P. s.* 'Leopard' has later deep rose flowers and the fiercest spots. Height 10in (25cm) and spread 24in (60cm). Zones 4-8.

PUSCHKINIA SCILLOIDES
Puschkinia
One of the prettiest early spring bulbs, carrying hyacinth-like bell stars loosely on a spike, if you're lucky, from early March. Once established it blossoms freely and looks wonderful with clumps of delphinium blue *Scilla siberica*.

P. s. var. *libanotica* 'Alba' is stunning, its small white clusters set off by vivid green upright leaves. Height 6in (15cm).

The white form is derived from *Puschkinia scilloides* plain and simple, the striped squill. The flowers are silver blue with deep Prussian blue veining down the centre of each petal. Its leaves tend to be more floppy, and perhaps less vivid. Both zone 4.

PYRACANTHA
Firethorn
A relation of cotoneaster, except that it has thorns and toothy leaves. Not my most favourite shrub in the world for that reason. It is most often grown against walls, and flowers and berries happily on north and east walls. They do well in any fertile soil, they don't mind sea breezes or high winds or industrial smog and with their pretty white hawthorn flowers and their red, orange or yellow autumn and winter berries, they are most amenable.

Apart from the thorns, they have one other drawback: they can be susceptible to fireblight and canker. *P. atalantioides*, for example, has nice flowers, glossy leaves, is happy with or without sun and has masses of scarlet berries. But it is very susceptible to the dreaded fireblight.

Try instead: 'Orange Glow' (shown above) or 'Navajo', raised at the US National Arboretum, Washington; it is resistant to fireblight, has small flattish berries, orange-red, which ripen late and hang on longer. 'Shawnee' has the same origins and is claimed to be resistant to both fireblight and scab. Abundant white flowers followed by yellow to pale orange fruits. All zones 5-6.

RHAMNUS
Buckthorn
A genus of about 125 species, deciduous or evergreen, grown as trees or shrubs, the buckthorn makes an extremely handsome alternative to holly – or indeed pyracantha and cotoneaster – for its profusion of berries. They grow in all soils in sun or semi shade. Their only disadvantage is the smell of their berries, so don't handle them.

R. alaternus, the Italian buckthorn, is a bushy, fast-growing evergreen shrub with dark green, shiny leaves and red berries going black with age. *R. a.* 'Angustifolia' is the hardier variety; *R. a.* 'Argenteovariegata' (shown above) has marbled green leaves with a cream margin and is very decorative on its own, even more so when sporting its red winter berries. It is amenable to clipping, though it naturally makes a 12ft (3.6m) pyramid if left to its own devices. It would prefer a wall, for it may need some shelter.

R. frangula, the alder buckthorn, makes a large shrub or a small tree, has nice yellow leaves in autumn and is perhaps the most ornamental with berries both red and black. A little known advantage is that its wood makes the best charcoal. So it's a must, obviously. Zone 7.

RHODODENDRON

Rhododendron

This genus produces some of the most magnificent and scented flowers in existence. In recent years it has been given a bad and often ignorant press – a sad case of inverted snobbery. All need neutral to acid soil.

R. arboreum was the first rhododendron to be introduced from the Himalayas and is the parent of the hardy hybrids. It flowers very early though its flowers, the reds especially, can be ruined by frost. To 40ft (12m) with a spread of 10ft (3m). Zones 6-9.

R. dauricum (shown above) is semi-evergreen but fully hardy and suitable for the small garden or container – especially in lime soil – with a height and spread of only 5ft (1.5m). It will flower in February or earlier with trusses of rose-purple. Zones 4-8.

R. mucronulatum is hardy, bears bright rose-mauve flowers January to March, is slender in habit and deciduous, height 6-10ft (1.8-3m). Zones 6-9.

R. Nobleanum is a hybrid group with rose red buds opening, ceteris paribus, from January in varieties of white, palest pink or a rich rose-red. Slow growing, height and spread to 15ft (4.5m), prefers a sheltered position. Zones 6-9.

RIBES

Currant

This is the family that produces redcurrants, blackcurrants and gooseberries. It includes the flowering currant, *R. sanguineum*, with its pink and red flowers in spring; and the buffalo currant, *R. odoratum*, which has fragrant gold, clove-scented flowers in spring.

R. laurifolium (shown above) is an evergreen early flowerer: in late winter it produces long racemes of pale green flowers which it might have borrowed from the common hop. It is a twiggy, spreading shrub. Zones 7-8.

ROSA

Rose

You will have your own favourites among roses but there are two reasons for choosing them for winter. One is that those that flower late will, in a mild winter and in a sheltered position, still be flowering at Christmas. And when it gets very cold, there is something beautiful about the pathos of a bloom iced with frost, an heroic death.

If you share this somewhat hysterical and fanciful approach to horticulture, seek out those that flower latest. I have seen the musk rose, 'Penelope', parchment coloured, but her layers of petals perfectly preserved under a heavy crystal frost, and *R.* x *odorata* 'Pallida' (syn. 'Old Blush China') still putting forth a mass of rose-pink frills against a sheltered wall at the end of December.

The other reason for roses is their hips. Their attraction for birds depends on the severity of the winter, internet info for birds and whether they have learned to love them. If they are starving you should feed them anyway. Good hips come from *R. eglanteria*, sweet briar and *R. glauca* with sprays of scarlet hips; *R. moyesii* with clusters of long vermilion hips and *R. virginiana* with fat red fruits. Zones 4-9.

ROSMARINUS

Rosemary

This is a lovely evergreen herb, a soft grey-green foil for early bulbs, good for clumps in gaps, good for paths and steps and good for the pot. As you brush past its long soft thin leaves, you will want to reach out and run them through your hand and absorb its sweet, dry, aromatic scent.

R. officinalis will grow bushy and dense with a height and spread of about 5ft (1.5m). 'Miss Jessopp's Upright' (shown above), happily for her, is erect with a height and spread to about 6ft (1.8m). It will make a good hedge if you are not fanatical about tidiness.

The only drawback to rosemary is that the flowers can tend to look rather washed out. The variety 'Benenden Blue' (syn. 'Collingwood Ingram') has clearly been on an assertiveness training course for it produces flowers a stronger blue than is usual. It will start flowering in winter if the weather has been kind and carry on into spring, with a renaissance if you are lucky in autumn. Zones 8-9.

RUBUS

Bramble

There is nothing quite so eerie as coming across the great white arcs of rubus, luminous on a cold clear night, at the far end of a vista across a frosted lawn. Whether you wish to grow it to unnerve friends and relations or to enjoy its fantastical symbolic aesthetic is for you to decide, but in either event it would detract from its power if you were to cosy it up to a lot of pretty-pretty flowering shrubs or suburbanise it with neatly edged borders.

R. biflorus, whose lattice of thick stems appears silver-white, is in fact pink-green overlaid with a waxy bloom. It has white flowers in early summer followed by yellow fruits which are edible. It can get up to 8ft (2.4m) with a final width of 13ft (4m) but, of course, you don't have to allow it to. Zone 7.

R. phoenicolasius (shown above), the Japanese wineberry, looks in winter as if it is about to make a hostile take-over bid with its exceedingly dramatic orange-red thorny stems arching in every direction. It is prudent to train it against a wall. The buds are green and covered in maroon bristles: they open green and look like the cut

section of a star fruit with a tiny white flower inside. The berries hang in clusters like under-ripe blackberries and are delicious, if few. Height to 8ft (2.4m), spread to 10ft (3m). Zone 6.

R. cockburnianus (shown above) is less geometrically rigid with arching thorny stems, their terracotta skin overlaid with a white, almost blue-white, bloom. The leaves, when they come, are a soft grey-blue-green and ferny; or alternatively you can try the yellow form, *R. c.* 'Golden Vale'. Height and spread to 15ft (4.5m) but very slowly. Zone 6.

SALIX
Willow

If willows were people they would be generous and graceful and unaware of it, being consumed by an overwhelming modesty and humility. Their long, narrow leaves in gentle falls are complaisant, accommodating themselves to the whims of the wind and the caprice of man, who will insist on coppicing and pollarding for a variety of reasons, aesthetic and practical. Even their very branches are pliant, as every basket weaver knows. But the willow has immense inner strength and will shrug off annual attempts at reconstruction, by putting out brave new shoots, often in glowing colour to warm your winter, and by hanging soft and furry catkins on its branches in spring.

If I have one prejudice against willows, it is against those that are small and weeping for they look rather sorry for themselves. The big weeping willows are fine, especially beside water. It is as if they have overcome their tendency to depression by a remarkable effort of will: magnificent through some deliberate generosity of spirit.

It is the first year stems that give you winter colour so in spring, before the leaves open, the willow must be cut well back. This is called coppicing if you grow it as a shrub, pollarding if a tree. Sadly, if you do this you will not get the catkins. Prioritise, grow both, or prune hard every other year.

S. alba vitellina 'Britzensis' (shown above left, syn. 'Chermensina'), the scarlet willow, for wands of fire. Appropriate pruning determines whether you keep it as a tree (up to 80ft or 24m) or a shrub (6ft or 1.8m). *S. a. vitellina*, (above) the golden willow, for egg yolk yellow stems. Zone 2.

S. daphnoides, the violet willow, for lovely violet stems overlaid with a white bloom. The female trees are narrow and columnar, the male trees have lavender catkins. As a tree it will get to about 15ft (4.5m) or can be kept as a shrub. Zone 5.

S. gracilistyla is a vigorous shrub with young charcoal grey stems and silky grey catkins barely concealing red, later yellow, anthers. *S. g.* 'Melanostachys' has very dark catkins and brick red, later yellow, anthers. Height to 10ft (3m). Zone 6. *S. irrorata* has dark purple stems in winter with a white bloom. The catkins begin red and end up yellow. Height to 10ft (3m). Zone 5.

SALVIA OFFICINALIS
Sage

Whilst you can overdo sage in the cooking pot, you can let it go in the garden as it is an extremely useful ornamental groundcover, growing to 2ft (60cm) with a spread of 3ft (90cm).

S. o. 'Berggarten' is a lovely, downy grey-green, very subtle. *S. o.* 'Purpurascens' is the most impressive, with young leaves of dark purple felt ageing to a maroon-green. In summer heat it bears spires of mauve flowers but is reluctant to flower in cold climes. Sage is essentially a Mediterranean plant so you need to give it a sunny place and dry to well-drained soil to get the best out of it.

There are many other variants such as *S. o.* 'Icterina', green and yellow variegated, and *S. o.* 'Tricolor', cream, green and pink, but showiness like this at ground level I find is too distracting. Zones 7-9.

SARCOCOCCA
Sweet box, Christmas box
This shrub looks nothing like box and it would be a mistake to think you could use it for any form of topiary. It is grown for its sweet winter fragrance emanating from its small, tatty flowerheads which look that way because the petals are insignificant: it is the anthers that you see. They are succeeded by berries, black, red or purple. It is especially good in chalk soils.

S. confusa: dense, spreading, glossy dark leaves, cream anthers, shiny black fruits and fragrant. Height and spread to 6ft (1.8m). S. hookeriana: upright but untidy, dense, white 'flowers' and black fruits. S. h. var. digyna (shown above): leaves of fresh green with pink-white flowers and black fruits, height and spread 3ft (1m). S. h. var. humilis: dwarf suckering variety rarely more than 2ft (60cm) high, good fragrance and grows well in shade. Pink anthers and black fruits.

S. orientalis: vigorous, upright with pink anthers and black fruits. S. ruscifolia: small and slow-growing and rather rare. Dark red berries. S. saligna: purple berries but the only one with little to no scent which would defeat the object of planting this shrub. Zones 6-9.

SCILLA
Squill
These are the wild hyacinths that produce tiny stars or hang their little, open bells downwards, both with great charm. The latter look like blue snowdrops and, in fact, they make a very pretty couple clumped together. You must be careful to match flowering times and heights.

S. bifolia has turquoise stars only 3in (8cm) high. S. siberica 'Atrocaerulea' has almost gentian-blue bells, is 4-6in (10-15cm) high and is lovely coupled with snowdrops. As is S. s. 'Spring Beauty', height 6in (15cm) in a deep bright china blue. More or less early spring bulbs, and certainly later than the following.

S. mischtschenkoana: open, upward looking faces full of enthusiasm, these are very early (January to March) silver blue stars, with a faint line of hyacinth blue down the centre of the petals. Several need to be planted together to make pretty little posies only 4in (10cm) high. They are good massed in a dish on an outdoor table where you can see them eye to eye, or naturalised in grass which people are unlikely to clump across. This species is too similar in colour to be effective with snowdrops. All zones 4-5.

SEDUM
Ice plant
One of the most useful perennials, with its attractive, glaucous, fleshy leaves making thick clumps, becoming higher and wider through the summer (height to 2ft or 60cm) until it begins to form flattish, rounded heads like a compressed cauliflower. This may not sound very attractive but I can assure you this is a fascinating plant. Sedum 'Herbstfreude' (syn. 'Autumn Joy') is one of the best. The heads begin a greenish ivory, turn buff, deepen to a dusty rose and thence to burgundy all autumn through.

Do not under any circumstances chop them off when they appear to be past their best. As winter gets underway they will blacken but look the more effective for it, especially under frost or against an expanse of snow.

They make rounded clumps of their own accord but I have seen them used effectively as the filling for rectangular beds edged in low box. Easily divided they will make a whole new mass next year. They are also irresistible to butterflies. Zone 4.

SKIMMIA
Skimmia

Evergreen shrubs with flowers or fruits for winter. The flowers are fragrant but not overwhelmingly so. They prefer an acid soil but most tolerate lime in a heavy soil. Mine do well in shade in a totally non-acid, heavy soil with tendencies to clay.

S. x confusa 'Kew Green' is a dome of shiny green aromatic leaves and large cones of scented cream flowers with gold anthers, produced between February and April. Height and spread to 4ft (1.2m). Zones 7-9.

S. japonica makes a mound of leathery leaves and clusters of white, sometimes fragrant flowers in late spring. *S. j.* ssp. *reevesiana* is a dwarf, lime hating form to 2ft (60cm). Clusters of white flowers in May produce crimson berries the winter through, lasting while the next season's flowers are produced. *S. j.* 'Nymans' is a free-fruiting female which needs a companion male plant to make the large bright red fruits. *S. j.* 'Veitchii' is shown above, while *S. j.* 'Rubella' sounds like something to be vaccinated against, especially with its cones of tight red nodules. But they open with fragrant white, pink flushed petals. Height and spread 2-3ft (60-90cm). Zones 7-8.

SORBUS
Rowan, mountain ash

Sorbus is a large and lovely family with a delicate ferny leaves and plenty of berries, irresistible to birds. How long the berries last is a function of the birds' hunger so if you provide a meal on the bird table you might save the berries for yourself.

S. cashmiriana (shown above) is a small open tree whose serrated foliage goes bronze in autumn and whose soft pink May flowers produce white berries long after the leaves have fallen. *S.* 'Chinese Lace' is also small with deeply cut, lacy foliage which turns maroon in fall. The berries are dark red. *S. commixta* has long winter sticky buds, glabrous leaves, copper in youth turning orange and red in autumn, and white spring flowers that produce fat scarlet berries for autumn. Zones 5-7.

S. hupehensis has purplish branches and glaucous leaves. This is a small tree of subtle colour except in late autumn when it turns red. The white, pink flushed fruits hang in drooping clusters into winter. *S. h.* var. *obtusa* has peach-pink fruits. Zone 6. *S.* 'Joseph Rock' for yellow berries (zone 5), *S. vilmorinii* for grey foliage, bronze-purple in autumn and clusters of rosy fruits. Zone 6.

STYRAX JAPONICUS
Snowbell

A most worthwhile investment, this is a small deciduous tree, alternatively grown as a large shrub, with a fan of glossy dark green leaves and a profusion of pendent white fragrant bells in summer. It transforms itself in winter when its branches produce a whizzing, whirling confusion which is best appreciated under a hoar frost.

S. j. 'Pink Chimes' (one of the Benibana Group which, in Japanese, means pink flowered) is the floriferous rosy version, with pale pink flowers flushed deeper at their core.

There are many other forms of styrax, including *S. officinalis*, again with fragrant drooping white bells; and *S. wilsonii* where the flowers hang as yellow-centred white skirts, but they do not produce the same burst of winter wizardry. They all positively hate lime. Zones 7-8.

SYMPHORICARPOS
Snowberry

Introduced from North America in the eighteenth century (although it has a relative in China) the snowberry is a deciduous shrub with insignificant flowers yet prolific berries, white or rose, which appear in autumn and last well into winter. For some reason, the fruits are unpalatable to birds.

S. albus is the white-berried form, after pink summer flowers, making a small shrub of slender downy shoots. *S. a.* var. *laevigatus* will make a thicket of blue-green stems and produce fistfuls of shining marbles. Height and spread to 6ft (1.8m).

From the Dutch-raised Doorenbos hybrids, 'Erect' is a vigorous, compact shrub with trusses of mauve-rose berries. In the same group you will find 'Mother of Pearl', eponymously named for its fruits, white flushed rose.

S. orbiculatus is the coralberry or Indian currant, which bears pink or white flowers in late summer and early autumn followed by round rose-purple fruits against the delicate tracery of its branches. Zones 3-6.

TAXUS
Yew, English yew

Indispensable for the multiplicity of its uses, the yew will make hedges, obelisks, pyramids, spheres, squirrels or any form you like. It is the staple of the topiarist's life.

Left to its own devices, this evergreen coneless conifer will make a large shrub or tree to 40ft (12m) with a spread of 30ft (9m). Yew makes an excellent hedge, its density affording the best of shelter and its sculptural potential means that you can use it as a formal backdrop, as part of the architecture of the garden, or as a decorative component. If you want its red berries you must get the female form. It is not as slow growing as is fabled. Established, it will do a minimum of 12in (30cm) a year.

You can get low prostrate forms for groundcover, spreading sweeping branched yews, gold yews and variegated yews. The best yew for a formal, columnar tree is the Irish or fastigiate yew, especially *T. b.* 'Fastigiata Robusta'; or 'Standishii' if you want a golden form. *T.* x *media* has several forms excellent for hedging: 'Brownii', 'Hatfieldii' and 'Sargentii'.

The foliage and seed within the red berry are highly poisonous. Zone 6.

TULIPA
Tulip

In general, the principle to follow is that the shorter the tulip, the earlier it is likely to flower. The elegance of the tall lily-flowered tulips, the great peony bowls, the green striped Viridiflora and the ostentatious ruffles of the parrot tulips, all must come later.

Content yourself with short stubby stems but have the pleasure of watching their flowers open wide on seeing the sun as early as February. *T. humilis* 'Violet Queen', the crocus tulip, a deep pink-violet globe only 4in (10cm) high, makes a good companion for real crocuses and dwarf iris; *I. danfordiae* is the same height and its colour brings out the bluish depths of the tulip.

Kaufmanniana tulips (shown above) are one of the most permanent. They do not have to be dug up or stored, but will come up year after year. These flower in March: 'Berlioz', a daffodil yellow opening to pale gold, 5in (12cm) high; 'Gaiety', a waterlily of rose outer petals and a creamy interior with a saffron throat, 6in (15cm) high; 'Heart's Delight' with carmine outer petals edged in palest pink, an ivory interior and golden throat, and purple slashed leaves. 8in (20cm).

VIBURNUM
Viburnum

A family of shrubs and trees useful at various times of the year, they may be deciduous, semi evergreen or evergreen. Good ones for the winter are as follows:

V. tinus (laurustinus) is evergreen and bushy with dark glossy leaves. As autumn progresses it makes clusters of florets, dark pink in bud, which open white through the winter. I have two which I have pruned into large well-behaved spheres atop stout single stems. It will make a height and spread of 10ft (3m) if you let it. I won't. Zone 8.

I also have *V.* x *bodnantense* 'Dawn' (shown above), deciduous but deliciously scented, with pale pink flowers appearing before the end of autumn and carrying on through winter. Oblivious to frost and snow, the rose pink buds, pink flowers, and far fragrance make it one of the best things about winter. Height 8ft (2.4m) ; Spread 6ft (2m). Zone 7.

V. farreri, a deciduous erect shrub and equally fragrant, has pink buds but white flowers. The leaves are bronze when young. Equally fragrant with pure white flowers through winter and pale spring foliage is *V. f.* 'Candidissimum'. For pink flushed flowers choose 'Farrer's Pink'. Zones 5-8.

VINCA
Periwinkle

This is a hardy trailing evergreen, remarkable because it always looks fresh whatever the season. There are lots of vincas, *major* and *minor*, and their most common use is as ground cover – they are highly effective weed smotherers. This is rather a waste, or an unimaginative use of the plant if it is kept for this purpose alone.

I keep my *Vinca major* 'Variegata', with its heart-shaped green leaves margined and flushed with ivory cream, in a long trough where it spills out over shallow steps. I also use it in urns and tubs in the winter where it replaces summer helichrysum. Its longevity is formidable: the vinca in the long trough has now been going for over 10 years. And it still bears pretty mauve-lilac flowers. Shown above is *V. minor* 'Argenteovariegata'. Zone 8.

YUCCA
Yucca

Exotic swords, these evergreen plants are like phormiums, and will make a winter garden look sub-tropical at any time of the year. Highly architectural, they are often used as punctuation marks at the corners of borders but in fact look just as good mixed with other planting. One of the most effective uses I have seen is in a row lining a short drive. Despite their exotic appearance they are quite hardy.

Y. filamentosa makes clumps of grey glaucous straps with curly white whiskers along the leaf edge. Erect in the centre, arching at the perimeter, it makes an eventual height and width of 5ft (1.5m). There are a number of variegated forms: 'Bright Edge' with a narrow gold margin, 'Variegata' with a cream-white margin. All produce ivory cream bells on upright stems of 3-6ft (1-1.8m) in July and August.

Y. flaccida is equally stemless with green or glaucous leaf and shorter flower stems. *Y. f.* 'Ivory' has ivory flowers flushed green.

Y. gloriosa has a stout stem and tufts of narrow blue-green leaves. Similar but arching is *Y. recurvifolia*, with a short stem and recurved leaves at its centre. Zones 5-9.

INDEX

Bold type denotes a major reference

Acer, **92**
Achillea, 70
Adonis, **92**
Agave americana 'Mediopicta', 62
Ajuga, **92**, 115
Alchemilla mollis, 23, 39
alder buckthorn, 120
alum root, 109
American aspen, 118
Amphlett, Rev. George
  l'Estrange, 26
Anemone, 49, **93**
  nemorosa, 105
Arbutus, **93**
Artemisia, **93**
  'Powis Castle', 58, 61
aspen, 118
Asplenium nidus, 105
Aster, 58
Atlantic cedar, 96
autumn cherry, 119
azalea, 65

bamboo, **94**
bay, 14, 65, 111
beech, 6, 11, 14, 20, 23, 77
Bergenia, **94**
  purpurascens, 39
  'Sunningdale', 57
Bethlehem sage, 119
Betula, 77, **94**
birch, 77, 94
Blechnum capense, 105
blue fescue, 105
box, 14, 17, 19, 34, 39, 62, 63,
  65, 66, 82, 95
bramble, 122
Brookes, John, 42
buckthorn, 120
bugle, 92
Bulbocodium vernum, 97
Buxus, **95**

Callicarpa bodinieri, **95**
Calluna vulgaris, 43, **95**
Camellia, 65, **96**
  sasanqua, 10
Carex, **96**
Catalpa bignonioides, 87
Ceanothus, 23, 24
cedar, 96
Cedrus, **96**
Chaenomeles, **97**
Chamaecyparis lawsoniana
  'Winston Churchill', 56
Charles I, 34
Charles II, 78
checker berry, 107
cherry tree, 119
Chimonanthus praecox, **97**
Chionodoxa, 49, **97**
Choisya, **98**

christmas box, 124
christmas rose, 108
Clematis, **98**
  'Gravetye Beauty', 106
Colorado spruce, 117
common spindle, 104
coralberry, 126
corkscrew hazel, 99
Cornus, **98**
  alba 'Elegantissima', 77
  'Kesselringii', 55, 57
  'Sibirica', 56
  sanguinea 'Winter Beauty',
    56, 57
  stolonifera 'Flaviramea', 54,
    57, 77
Corsican pine, 118
Cortaderia, **99**
  selloana 'Pumila', 61
Corylopsis, **99**
Corylus, **99**
Cotoneaster, **100**
crab apple, 114
Crocus, 49, 51, 97, **100**, 112
Culpeper, Thomas, 37
Cupressus, **101**
Cyclamen, 49, 51, 65, 97, **101**
cypress, 101

daffodil, 42, 46, 49, 65, 66, 115
Daphne, **101**
delphinium, 24
Dicksonia antarctica, 105
dog's tooth violet, 103
dogwood, 77, 98
Douglas fir, 118

Edgeworthia crysantha, **102**
Elaeagnus, **102**
  pungens 'Maculata', 43, 45,
    56, 57
Elizabeth I, 34
English yew, 126
Eranthis, 45, 46, 49, **102**
Erica, 43, **103**
  erigena 'Irish Dusk', 55
Erysimum 'Bowles' Mauve', **103**
Erythronium, **103**
Eucalyptus, **104**
Euonymus, **104**
  fortunei 'Silver Queen', 54, 57
Euphorbia, 74, **104**

Fagus 6, 14, 20, 23
  sylvatica 'Purpurea Pendula',
    11, 77
Fargesia nitida, 94
ferns, 23, 74, **105**
Festuca glauca, **105**
firethorn, 120
flowering currant, 121
Forsythia, **106**

fragrant winterhazel, 99

Galanthus, **106**
Garrya elliptica, 74, **106**
Gaultheria, **107**, 116
giant butterbur, 116
glory of the snow, 49, 97
grape hyacinth, 114
gum tree, 104

Hakonechloa, **107**
Hamamelis, **107**
  x *intermedia* 'Jelena', 55
hardiness zones, 91
hazel, 99
heather, 42, 43, 55, 103, 114
Hebe, **108**
  'Red Edge', 11
Hedera, **108**
  helix, 'Oro di Bogliasco', 16, 77
hedges, 14, 34, 70, 87
hellebore, 42, 45, 108
Helleborus, **108**
  foetidus, 42
  orientalis, 45, 92, 115
Henry VIII, 34
Hepatica, **109**
Heuchera, **109**
Hicks, David, 19
Himalayan birch, 94
holly, 19, 110
honesty, 91, 113
hornbeam, 34
Howard, Catherine, 37
Hyacinthus, **109**
Hydrangea, 23, 24, 88

ice plant, 124
Ilex, **110**
  x *altaclerensis* 'Golden King', 19
Indian currant, 126
Iris, 49, **110**
  danfordiae, 6
Italian buckthorn, 120
Itea ilicifolia, 86, 87
ivy, 62, 77, 108

Japanese apricot, 119
Japanese larch, 111
Japanese quince, 97
Japanese wineberry, 122
japonica, 97
Jasminum nudiflorum, **110**
Jekyll, Gertrude, 58
juniper, 42, 111
Juniperus, **111**
  chinensis 'Kuriwao Gold', 11

Kent, William, 82, 84
King, Miles, 51

laburnum tunnel, 33
lady's mantle, 23, 39
Lamium galeobdolon
  'Hermann's Pride', 86, 87
Larix kaempferi, **111**
Laurus, **111**
laurustinus, 127
lenten rose, 108
Leucojum, **112**

lime, 20, 23, 30, 39
ling, 95
liverwort, 109
Lonicera, 87, **112**
Lunaria annua, 91, **113**
lungwort, 119

MacLeod Matthews, Col.
  and Mrs, 34
Magnolia, **113**
Mahonia, 43, 45, **113**
Makepeace, John, 13
Malus, **114**
maple, 92
Mexican orange blossom, 98
mezereon, 101
milkweed, 104
Miscanthus, 58, 61, **114**
mountain ash, 125
Muscari, 66, **114**

Narcissus, 114, **115**
  'February Gold', 42
  'Tête à Tête', 65
New Zealand flax, 117
Noel, Anthony, 16, 17, 62-66

old man's beard, 98
oleaster, 102
Ophiopogon, **115**
Oregon grape, 113
ornamental cabbage, 17, 66
Oryzopsis, 52, 57
Osmanthus, **115**

pampas grass, 61, 99
paper bark maple, 92
Parrotia persica, **116**
partridge berry, 107
perennial wallflower, 103
periwinkle, 127
peony, 24
Pennisetum alopecuroides, 58, 61
Pernettya, **116**
Persian ironwood, 116
Petasites, **116**
Peto, Harold, 78
Phoenix roebelenii, 88
Phormium, 58, 61, **117**
Phyllostachys, 94
Picea, **117**
Pieris japonica, **117**
Pinus, **118**
Pleioblastus variegatus, 94
Polypodium cambricam, 105
  vulgare 'Cornubiense', 105
Polystichum munitum, 105
Populus tremula, **118**
primrose, 118
Primula vulgaris, **118**
Prunus, **119**
  laurocerasus 'Zabeliana', 77
  serrula, 10, 43
Pulmonaria, **119**
Puschkinia scilloides, 92, **120**
Pyracantha, **120**

Rasch, Lady Anne, 78
Rhamnus, **120**
Rhododendron, 65, **121**

Ribes, **121**
Rosa, 80, 81, **121**
  'Felicia', 69, 81
  'Lady Hillingdon', 23
Rose, 24, 39, 70, 73, 82, 121
Rosemary, 122
Rosmarinus, **122**
rowan, 125
Rubus, **122**
  thibetanus, 52, 55

sage, 58, 123
Salix, **123**
  'Erythroflexuosa', 52, 55
Salvia officinalis, **123**
  purpurea, 20, 23
Sarcococca, 66, **124**
Scilla, 46, 48, **124**
  bithynica, 46
  siberica, 120
Scots pine, 118
sedge, pendulous, 96
Sedum, 61, **124**
  'Herbstfreude', 58
silk tassel bush, 106
silver grass, 114
Skimmia, 65, 66, **125**
snake bark maple, 92
snowbell, 125
snowberry, 126
snowdrop, 41, 45, 46, 49, 51, 106
snowflake, 112
Sorbus, **125**
spurge, 104
spruce, 117
Stachys byzantina, 24
statuary, 15, 82, 84
strawberry tree, 93
Strong, Sir Roy, 14
Styrax japonicus, 74, 77, **125**
Swedish birch, 94
sweet box, 124
Symphoricarpos, **126**

Taxus baccata, **126**
  'Fastigiata', 26
Thompson, Sir Edward and
  Lady, 26, 28
Tilia platyphyllos 'Rubra', 20
topiary, 13, 26-29, 34
traveller's joy, 98
Tulipa, 34, **126**

valerian, 24
veronica, 108
Verey, Rosemary, 19
Viburnum, **127**
Vinca, **127**

willow, 81, 123
windflower, 93
winter aconite, 45, 46, 49, 102
winter-flowering jasmine, 110
winter heliotrope, 116
wintersweet, 97
witch hazel, 55, 107
wormwood, 93

yew, 13, 26, 30, 34, 70, 126
Yucca, **127**